HOMEGROWN

A GROWING GUIDE *for* CREATING *a*
COOK'S GARDEN *in* RAISED BEDS, CONTAINERS,
and SMALL SPACES

MARTA TEEGEN

Rodale books may be purchased for business or promotional use or for special sales. For information, please write to: Special Markets Department, Rodale Inc., 733 Third Avenue, New York, NY 10017.

Printed in the United States of America

Rodale Inc. makes every effort to use acid-free ⊗, recycled paper ♻.

Book design by Joanna Williams

Illustrations by Lizzie Harper, www.lizzieharper.co.uk

Library of Congress Cataloging-in-Publication Data
Teegen, Marta.
    Homegrown : a growing guide for creating a cook's garden / Marta Teegen.
        p.   cm.
    ISBN-13 978-1-60529-517-6 hardcover
    ISBN-10 1-60529-517-5 hardcover
    1. Vegetable gardening. 2. Kitchen gardens. I. Title.
SB320.9.T44 2010
635—dc22   2010009022

Distributed to the trade by Macmillan

2 4 6 8 10 9 7 5 3 1 paperback

We inspire and enable people to improve their lives and the world around them

For more of our products visit **rodalestore.com** or call 800-848-4735

For my father

·CONTENTS·

Introduction   vii

Chapter 1 Garden of Eden   1
Chapter 2 Location   7
Chapter 3 Raised Beds and Containers   14
Chapter 4 Creating Amazing Soil   21
Chapter 5 Seeds, Seedlings, and Planting   34
Chapter 6 A Gallery of Plants and Amazing Produce   50
Chapter 7 Maintaining the Garden   108
Chapter 8 Controlling Pests and Diseases   116
Chapter 9 Caring for the Garden Off-Season   127
Chapter 10 Seasonal Recipes and Menus   133

Resources   175
Recommended Reading   177
Acknowledgments   178
Index   179

INTRODUCTION

What Is a Front-Yard Farm?

The year before I started my kitchen garden design business, Homegrown LA, I was living on a hilltop in the Mt. Washington neighborhood of Los Angeles, between downtown and Pasadena. I had recently returned from 6 months of study with home cooks in India and was eager to continue to work with food, but I knew that the long hours and low pay of restaurant work and catering or being a freelance home chef was not for me—because I'd already done all of those things.

In thinking about my future, I decided to convert my front yard into a vegetable garden. Although I had spent time on my family's farms as a child, I didn't consider myself a gardener. I'm a cook first, and I know the pleasures of fresh produce. But I knew that I was interested in growing many of the vegetables I had learned to cook with and had seen at the farmers' markets in Los Angeles.

My first kitchen garden in LA was a little over 200 square feet in size and included heirloom varieties from A to Z (well, to W, to be truthful). It was an ambitious project, and it taught me many things about planting, spacing, harvesting, and, most of all, appreciating the flavors and textures of just-picked vegetables and herbs.

WHAT I GREW IN MY FIRST KITCHEN GARDEN

My first garden included these vegetables: artichokes, arugula, beets, bell peppers, broccoli, cabbage, cantaloupe, carrots, cauliflower, celery, chile peppers, cucumbers, eggplants, endive, Florence fennel, garlic, green beans, leeks, lettuce, onions, peas, potatoes, pumpkins, radicchio, radishes, shallots, sorrel, soybeans, spinach, strawberries, sweet corn, Swiss chard, tomatoes, upland cress, and watermelon.

And these herbs: basil, chives, cilantro, dill, marjoram, mint, oregano, parsley, rosemary, sage, tarragon, and thyme.

And these edible flowers: borage, calendula, nasturtiums, sunflowers, and violets.

I quickly realized that I liked having daily access to fresh greens and herbs, both for salads and for cooking. Tomatoes and melons were also a definite treat. Consequently, my garden was transformed into a salad garden after that first year, with a melon patch alongside.

In my eyes, the plants in my garden produce ingredients for meals, and I spend much more time choosing what to harvest on a given day than I spend actually cooking. By being in the garden for a few minutes every day, I can easily see when it's time to gather my homegrown bounty at its peak of freshness.

Soon after my garden was planted, I began throwing regular dinners for friends, building menus that featured the produce from my impressively reliable front-yard farm. It was surprisingly simple and, as a cook, an ongoing source of inspiration and play. I was no longer teasing out an elusive nuance of flavor from a vegetable that had been picked too early; I was now working in a palate of bold tastes and textures, colors, and shapes with produce picked at its peak and potential.

Then I began to get requests to design similar kitchen gardens for families and friends throughout the city—so Homegrown LA was born.

The vegetable gardens I design come in a variety of shapes, sizes, and colors, but they all share distinctive qualities. They are consistently and predictably productive while also visually entrancing, exuding a dreamy exuberance that suggests the romantically unkempt gardens of rural French villages.

My intensively planted gardens are designed to take root in spaces usually off-limits to vegetables, such as weedy nooks, tangled corners, and front yards. There are only two basic requirements—adequate sun and nutrient-rich soil. The results are impressive and well within your reach. With *Homegrown* as your guide, you simply choose the vegetables (and herbs and edible flowers!) you like to eat, create easy-care garden beds and containers, tend to your plants as they grow, and harvest your bounty for delicious meals every day. You'll discover that kitchen gardening is rewarding beyond measure, both for you as a gardener and for you as a lover of organic, fresh, and flavor-filled dishes.

Marta Teegen

· 1 ·

GARDEN OF EDEN

What looks good today?

It's a simple enough question when you're at the market, running your fingers over a tomato, subtly squeezing it, and wondering if that waxy sheen is natural or not. It's markedly more complicated when you're shopping for food to serve at an organic restaurant.

One of my restaurant jobs took me to the aisles of the Santa Monica farmers' market, looking for both the staples and the exotic items, mentally keeping track of the changes we would need to make to the menu based on what was perfectly ripe that day.

In my world, my garden, and my kitchen, something is either ready to eat, at the peak of its freshness, or it's not.

It's that simple.

Unfortunately, this is not the case in the produce sections of most supermarkets. There, ripeness is a subjective term, and any appearance of ripeness may be a mere gilding of the lily, as maturity is not actually achieved but rather is applied through the processes of industrial food production. Veggies are taken from the field still green and are then sprayed with chemical showers to protect their skin, speed up coloration, and delay spoilage.

From the cook's point of view, there is no comparison between fresh from the garden and fresh from the grocery store bag. If you don't have the best-quality ingredients to work with, it doesn't matter what you're doing with them: The results will always be average. Once you are able to eat food at peak ripeness after growing it perfectly yourself, you'll never go back to the grocery store.

As a kitchen garden designer, I have developed a few guiding principles: Prepare your garden based on what you eat, have good materials at the start, look to nature as your guide for both diversity and design, and—like nature—be patient as well as ruthless.

PLANT WHAT YOU EAT

It is essential to remember that the goal is to plant your garden based on your eating habits and then to plan meals based on what is harvestable at any given time. While you may have to wait through a long summer to harvest the first Charentais melon, the sweetness of its flesh, still warm from the sun, is incomparable. As I patiently wait for my tomatoes to mature, I enjoy a salad of mixed lettuces, arugula, chives, dill, marjoram, parsley, sorrel, and upland cress. And when my tomatoes do come in, my basil will be at least 2 feet tall, which means I can finally make pasta with fresh tomato sauce that's seasoned with fresh basil I've picked myself.

Ask yourself: What do you like to eat fresh? What do you eat again and again? What grows easily in your backyard microclimate? For me, it is very special to have daily access to fresh greens. This is my personal preference, and it's the reason I can always build a meal around what's in my garden, 50 feet from my kitchen. My first year, I planted a very wide variety of vegetables just to see what would work and what I wanted. I slowly pared that back to mostly cooking greens, salad greens, melons, and tomatoes.

But don't think only in terms of individual vegetables—tomatoes or cucumbers, for example—but rather in terms of cuisines. While an Italian garden may include basil, eggplant, garlic, onions, oregano, pepperoncini, pole beans, red bell peppers, rosemary, sage, Swiss chard, and San Marzano tomatoes, an Asian garden may include bok choy, broccoli,

---

DEFINITIONS

Intensive planting, interplanting, companion planting. These three terms describe three techniques for planting within the microclimate of your garden. *Intensive planting* means spacing plants close together and allowing them to overlap, sometimes even crowding each other significantly. *Interplanting* is the practice of planting between plants, although not necessarily as closely as you'd find in intensive plantings. *Companion planting* is selecting and planting together plants that have a beneficial impact on each other or the plants around them.

---

cabbage, carrots, chile peppers, cilantro, cucumbers, eggplants, garlic, mustard, radishes, scallions, snow peas, soybeans, and yard-long beans. Such cuisine-based gardens overlap in some ways but are distinctly different in others. Happily, they can coexist, bringing variety not only to your garden but also to your kitchen and, ultimately, to your plate.

THE RIGHT MATERIALS: RAISED BEDS, GOOD SOIL, AND THE FRENCH INTENSIVE METHOD

The French intensive method, in brief, is a style of gardening that is designed to produce the greatest yields possible in a small area. It is organic and focused on maintaining soil health over successive seasons. Many of the aspects of what is now called the biointensive method (or simply "intensive") were used by ancient cultures around the world, from China to Greece to southern Mexico. It first took on a "scientific" mantle in 17th-century Paris, when it was popularized as a way of utilizing small spaces in ways that greatly

PLANT INTENSIVELY. With intensive planting, let nature be your guide for a beautiful, full, and abundant garden.

increased yields. Jean-Baptiste de La Quintinie, the head gardener to the Sun King, Louis XIV, is credited with systemizing this method for growing vegetables in an intensive manner, crowding the plantings in a closed system and relying upon horse manure to satisfy the nutritional demands of the gardens.

Your garden should begin with the right growing medium, as well as the right container. In some parts of the country, especially in the Midwest, excellent topsoil is a given—it's more the luck of the zip code than the luck of the draw. In Los Angeles and most other urban settings, however, yard soil can be clean fill or clay, and it may be rife with diseases or laced with long-outlawed pesticides, herbicides, or lead-based paints. Amending this type of soil is easier said than done; it often requires extensive laboratory tests and is much more complicated than simply scattering the soil with the proper amendments and digging them in, hoping for a miraculous reversal of problems with drainage, mineral depletion, and a lack of nutrients.

The solution I discovered, somewhat by accident, was to create a medium of stable bedding consisting of composted horse manure, wood shavings, and straw, amended with bonemeal and greensand and contained within raised beds of varying sizes. These are "growing-only, no-walking" areas that encourage extensive healthy root growth and limit soil compaction; they also allow more thorough and uniform drainage. While the raised beds can be made out of a variety of materials, from recycled concrete to brick to stone, I use inexpensive, untreated cedar boards that slip together with mortise and tenon joints, held in place by a wooden peg. Raised beds eliminate the heavy work that's often recommended when you start a new garden, such as double-digging soil a foot or more down to remove rocks, roots, and the inescapable accumulated detritus of an urban plot of land.

Remember: This isn't just about landscaping. It's about eating, and the objective is really twofold: to grow great ingredients for your kitchen—quickly, reliably, and efficiently—while at the same time growing great soil for your future plantings. You'll achieve the second objective through easy crop rotation (such as by alternately planting a cover crop or letting the soil rest through a season and planting appropriately the following year), adding amendments, and topping off the bed with a 1- to 2-inch layer of compost from your bins every growing season.

LOOKING TO NATURE

You may think that nature is the guiding force in many gardens. Seems obvious, right? Unfortunately, that's not the case. The "normal" vegetable garden today is very much a man-made phenomenon; there is nothing natural about tidy rows of plants positioned on top of tilled soil that's treated with chemical herbicides and pesticides and synthetic fertilizers. And the additives used in commercial farming were designed to increase harvests without concern for their impact on the environment, human health, or even the taste of the foods they produce.

It's a much better plan to emulate the natural landscape—just look to the local hillside, where there is a great mixture of plants competing for space. Those unlandscaped swaths of land, completely covered with a wide variety of plants standing cheek by jowl, should be your models. When plants have to literally struggle and fight with one another for their nutrients, air, and water, they're going to be stronger as a result. The intensive method I promote incorporates as much nature as possible into this process and calls for a diverse mix of plants in the kitchen garden, including vegetables, flowers, and herbs. This will create a healthy ecosystem where plants will thrive.

It may be hard to let go of what you think a vegetable patch is supposed to look like. But consider the way plants grow in nature—they're not in tidy rows. Your plants don't need wide spaces between them. I never have weeds in my gardens because weeds can't get a foothold—there is literally no room for them to grow. Weeds should never come up in an intensively planted garden. The goal is to have little to no soil surface exposed so there is no opportunity for weeds to grow.

While nature may be your guide in terms of diversity and density, you'll need to make your mark on the garden by deciding which plants earn their keep. The garden is not a democracy where the weak have to be protected from the strong. I am very interested in getting the best produce possible in the shortest amount of time, so if this goal is being stymied by bugs or disease, I'm ruthless—just like nature. If I have an aphid infestation, I'm likely to pull out the plant that's fallen victim and start over rather than nurse and baby it along. The point of growing vegetables is to eat them, and if a certain crop or variety is consuming my precious time because I have to coddle it, it will not be in my garden for long. My garden is filled with potential ingredients, but they are destined either for the kitchen or the compost bin, regardless. Ideally, you won't have many problems, as organic gardening tends to enable healthy plants rather than protect sick ones.

At the same time, be patient. It takes time for the miracle of photosynthesis to work its magic. Farmers plan seasons in advance; it's how they've survived since civilization began. Produce is available at farmers' markets year-round because it was grown in hothouses by growers forcing their vegetable plants during an off-season or using artificial lighting to encourage growth.

It takes time to grow food. Be patient and consistent. Visit your garden every day. Observe and participate.

Remember what this is all about—having amazing produce to cook with. Growing at home means your vegetables are picked when they are fully ripe and are eaten in season. You'll have access to the most tender and remarkable varieties—ones that commercial farmers and farmers' market growers won't grow because they'd never make it to market without spoiling.

Once harvested, let the food speak for itself; manipulate it as little as possible so it keeps its original taste and texture. This is my preferred way to cook and, not surprisingly, my preferred way to garden.

And finally, realize that this can and should be a beautiful experience, from garden to plate. One of my students is also a very gifted flower grower. She could never come to terms with having a vegetable garden because, in her words, they were always so "ugly"—these tidy rows of food just sitting in the ground. After the first season of growing in her intensively planted raised bed, she told me that it had never occurred to her that you could grow food with flowers and herbs mixed right in, or that such a garden could be so full and abundant.

Beautiful, full, abundant herbs and flowers. Throw in heirloom vegetables, and that's my Garden of Eden.

· 2 ·

LOCATION

My current garden is located on the patio of a fourth-floor apartment about 3 miles from downtown Los Angeles. The raised beds were here when I arrived and are deeper than I'd like, but they face south and get lots of residual heat from the hard surfaces around them. This is where I have my demonstration garden for students. It is long and narrow, and it's planted with a good mix of both edible and nonedible flowers, as well as vegetables and herbs.

While it doesn't compare to the 200 square feet of raised beds I started out with in my first garden in Mt. Washington, California, my small patio, despite being in an apartment building, turns out to be a perfect location for a kitchen garden. Indeed, I'm able to produce enough food here for two people, every day.

The very first step to creating your kitchen garden is determining the best location. Many of my clients initially think that they either don't have room for a garden or, if they do, they assume that it will be tucked away out of sight in the backyard, like an old-fashioned vegetable patch. Actually, a garden designed in the French intensive method uses a very small amount of space and is also pleasing to the eye, so there's no reason not to put it right up front, where everyone will see it.

There are three primary factors to consider when choosing the location for your kitchen garden: sunlight, water, and ease of access. Vegetables and herbs require a minimum of 6 hours of direct sun each day. A salad garden will tolerate more shade and is definitely the best choice for locations that only get morning sun. The kitchen garden should be located in an area that's easy to get to, with a hose or spigot nearby so watering and harvesting aren't a chore.

If the prime site for your kitchen garden is the front yard, clearly visible to the entire world, take advantage of the opportunity to show off both your design sensibilities and your culinary aesthetics. The variety of colors, shapes, and sizes possible in an intensively planted bed can provide a strikingly beautiful addition to the looks of your home. Think artichokes, borage, chives, Florence fennel, lavender, Swiss chard, and so on. All can easily do double duty as ornamentals and edible plants.

CREATIVE USE OF SPACE

If you have very restricted space to work with, you will need to think creatively and may have to break up the vegetable garden into several smaller areas rather than have one unified patch. One of my specialties is finding space for a garden where you can't possibly imagine there being room for one. I have put salad greens on a front stoop that is shaded in the afternoon, and I've run vegetables in long, narrow planters along the foundation on the south side of a house, rather than placing square or rectangular beds in the backyard where the owners' dogs and children play. So long as you think creatively, you will be able to figure out a good location for your veggies and herbs.

A kitchen garden could literally be one pot of mixed herbs or a series of pots going down your front steps. Fire escapes and windowsills are all possible garden spots. Take advantage of outdoor wall space by planting vegetables that can be trained to grow vertically to maximize yield in just a few square feet.

If you are gardening on a rooftop, it is very important to first confirm that your roof can support the weight of a garden by checking with the landlord or an engineer—raised beds, pots, and wet soil are all very heavy. You will also need to consider drainage and watering when growing on your roof, and that may require the expertise of an engineer or a plumber.

GROW VERTICALLY. When you grow vertically, you make the most of limited space by planting naturally climbing vegetables, such as cucumbers and pole beans, along fences and walls.

Container gardening is a great alternative when you don't have room for a larger raised bed. This means planting in spaces that may not be obvious but that exist in and around the house. Most vegetables can be grown in pots that are at least 10 inches in diameter. (Herbs need 6-inch pots.) An entire salad garden can be planted in a 12-inch round pot. It will only feed two people, but that pot will support arugula, chives, four different types of lettuce, marjoram, nasturtiums, flat leaf parsley, and sorrel. They'll all fit into and thrive in one pot.

In general, it's best to have everything in as few areas as possible, especially if you are hand watering. It's easier to keep track of your veggies and herbs if they are grown near one another, rather than spread out in multiple gardens around the house, so plan before you plant.

If you're gardening in a space that's not currently green (if it's surrounded by pavement, for example), you'll need to include a variety of flowering plants—in addition to your vegetables and herbs—to attract pollinating and beneficial insects. Any of the perennial salvias (the nonculinary kind) would be good additions.

SALAD IN A POT. A 12-inch round pot will produce a good mix of salad greens, flowers, and herbs.

No matter what site you're considering, it is important to draw a plan of your garden on paper before you start planting. You will want to place paths and underground irrigation (if you have that option) first, and then add your raised beds or containers. If you're planting directly on top of a lawn, it is not necessary to remove the turf, though you will need to put down a $1/2$-inch-thick layer of newspapers before adding your soil and plants. (This will keep grass from finding its way into your garden.)

SUNLIGHT

There is one golden rule for figuring out a location for your garden: Find the sunniest spot. You need to put your garden somewhere that gets a minimum of 6 hours of sun per day to grow most vegetables. Tomatoes want even more—up to 8 hours per day.

What is the sunlight like at your house? Where is it sunniest for the longest time? Surprisingly, many people can't answer this, so I always set up my first meeting with a client for midday, when the sun is at its highest. At times I'm told that they want the garden in the darkest, most horrible little mud spot in the back, often because it's the only place in the entire yard—front, back, or side—that isn't landscaped. I have to explain that there's no reason to spend the money to build a garden in that location, because it won't thrive.

Be realistic when deciding on a site. Generally speaking, most people don't have a spot that gets 6 full hours of sun. Even if you think you do, you need to monitor your sun for an entire day to confirm it; you may be surprised to find that some of that wonderful sunshine is blocked by trees, shrubs, the house, or a fence for part of the day. When I was living in Mount Washington, growing on the top of a hill where there was direct overhead sun all day long, I never had to use shade cloth, even at the height of summer, because the majority of my summer vegetables thrived in the sun, and my more delicate greens were shaded by my trellised beans. A container garden in full sun that is also surrounded by hard, reflective surfaces will work for some plants, but it won't for others. Tomatoes and melons will love the residual heat given off at night and the reflected heat of the day, and they'll prosper, but delicate salad greens will never be happy in that kind of situation.

I recently visited a home where the sunniest part of the yard was a small triangle next to a fence; the area drained into a patch of hillside-stabilizing California buckeye, chaparral, and manzanita, all of which are native plants. While the sunny location was perfect for a vegetable bed, the owner was worried about having water from the beds drain into the natives, which prefer drier conditions. Because of this, I suggested planting grapes, rather than vegetables, to take advantage of the location. The owner still benefits from homegrown produce, and the grapes like the heat, like to trail, and love the well-drained soil conditions.

WATER

There is really no way around it—vegetable plants require regular watering in order to develop amazing produce. And while there are ways to reduce your watering needs, such as by intensively planting your garden, you will nevertheless need a reliable source of water nearby.

Ask yourself these questions: Does the spot selected for your garden have a hose nearby? Will it be easy to carry a full watering can to your garden? You'll be watering frequently, so be sure to locate or create a water source, or commit yourself to carrying water. You should also check to see if there is an underground irrigation system installed in the area, such as lawn or flowerbed sprinklers that will need to be capped or redirected away from the vegetable garden.

Adequate drainage is a must for vegetable and herb beds. Beds placed on any nonporous surface—such as asphalt or concrete driveways, brick patios, and sealed decks—will tend to build up humidity underneath and consequently won't perform as well as they should. Humidity and excess moisture set the stage for diseases, mold, pests, and rot. A bed placed upon an asphalt driveway is also likely to develop dry and wet spots throughout due to uneven drainage. If we've exhausted all options for finding another location and must place the bed on asphalt or concrete, I'll either line the bottom of the bed with a 1-inch layer of pebbles or river rock, or I'll lift the bed slightly off the hard surface to allow water to drain away—but I only do this when I'm certain that the area can accommodate the extra weight. There is another, more labor-intensive solution, as well: Break up a concrete area and stack the broken concrete pieces to construct the beds themselves.

EASE OF ACCESS

In addition to sun and water, the accessibility of the garden is also an important consideration. If your garden is difficult to get to or far away from your house, the daily 10 to 15 minutes needed for proper maintenance will feel like a burden, rather than a joy.

If you're lucky enough to have multiple options when choosing where to plant your kitchen garden, choose the one closest to your house. Ideally, it would be situated right outside your kitchen door, and if it's planted intensively and maintained well, it will be as beautiful and welcoming as any ornamental bed you can plant. Remember, the closer the garden is, the more likely you are to spend time in it, which is especially important if you are watering by hand. At the height of the growing season, you should be in your garden every day, checking to see which vegetables are nearly ripe, which herbs are mature enough to harvest, and which plants need attention. You want the garden to be a place you want to come to—just a few steps away and definitely not out of sight. And part of the idea of ease of access is that you need to be able to carry your bumper crops (like cucumbers, melons, and squash) back up to your house easily.

ADDITIONAL CONSIDERATIONS

While most animal pests can be dealt with by using fencing or lining the bottoms of your raised beds with wire mesh, rodents can be a real problem, especially for urban gardeners. If there are badly maintained compost piles or trees that drop fruit nearby, choose another site if one is available. Many rodents can chew through or climb over any sort of protective barrier. I had to talk one client out of a location because there were mature avocado trees in the yard next door. It was rat central back there, and there were no cats or other predators to keep the population in check. In an urban setting, unless you're able to set traps throughout the yard, a garden can be eaten overnight.

Wind may also be a factor on your site, especially if you have a wide-open space or are on a hillside. Raised beds and containers that are exposed to regular winds face conditions that stress the plants, primarily through dehydration. This is important to consider, especially when containers are on a roof, balcony, or any other location that receives high winds, such as on the edge of a canyon or arroyo. If possible, try to locate your garden in an area protected from wind. If that's not possible, one solution might be to plant a row of ornamental grasses or shrubs running the length of your garden to act as a windbreak, though be sure they do not also block the sun from your garden.

If you plan on composting or starting your plants from seed, you should set aside space for each of these activities near your kitchen garden. It will be much easier to transport your compost to your beds if your composter is nearby. Likewise, having tables nearby for your seedlings means that they will be raised off the ground while hardening off before planting (see page 44). They'll also be protected from animals that might dig up their roots or unpot them.

TOOLS

In general, I believe less is better. I always have a few basic tools with me in the garden, including pruning shears, a hoe, and a watering wand. Pruning shears come in handy for both maintaining my garden and harvesting my veggies. I use a hoe when I'm preparing a new bed, and I use a long-arm watering wand to get water to all areas of the bed.

If you need to buy a hose, look for a high-quality, weather-resistant one in the shortest length possible to get the job done. Other tools you may find useful are weather-resistant plant labels and a permanent marker, bamboo or wooden stakes for making trellises and teepees, garden wire and string for supports, a shovel, a digging fork, and a rake.

If you plan to compost, you'll want at least one container with a lid. If you have room, the ideal setup includes two containers that each hold a minimum of 1 cubic yard of material (3 feet x 3 feet x 3 feet). If you plan on starting your plants from seed, you'll need seed trays and small pots. And if you have the room and accessible downspouts, it's great to have at least one barrel in which to collect rainwater. (Make sure the one you choose has a childproof lid.)

· 3 ·

RAISED BEDS AND CONTAINERS

Just as you can't grow a kitchen garden without sun, I don't recommend using my style of intensive gardening without raised beds or containers. While Jean-Baptiste de La Quintinie's system relied greatly on trench beds carved out of the soil for the Sun King's kitchen garden at Versailles, what you'll learn in *Homegrown* requires far less effort.

Remember: This is not in-ground gardening, but rather raised bed and container gardening that tailors the level of investment, effort, difficulty, and potential to suit the size of your family. Not everybody is gardener to the king, nor do we have legions of skilled gardeners laboring on our behalf.

For La Quintinie, intensive growing was the most reliable and versatile way to produce sufficient quantities of the food needed for everything from midnight snacks to state dinners. In my case, when I planted my first kitchen garden, I just wanted some fresh herbs to cook with and to see what vegetables might grow in my microclimate. Since growing in the hard-packed ground of Mount Washington was not an option, I built up instead, sowing all my vegetable dreams within four raised beds, each one 10 feet long, 5 feet wide, and 12 inches deep. They were too wide, I soon learned, since the center was hard to get to without nearly climbing into the bed, wrecking the soil by compacting it. I had to plant all the tall perennials that I didn't need regular access to in the middle, since it was the least-reachable place.

Despite this one small design problem, my gardens performed beyond my wildest expectations.

There are several advantages to growing in raised beds: First, you can easily control the content of the soil mix so it remains loose and fertile, and you never compact the soil because you do not walk on it. Both of these mean that roots are allowed to grow freely and are therefore strong enough to support the weight of a good yield. Second, plants grow better because the soil in raised beds warms slightly earlier than the ground does in spring, so you can plant earlier. Third, the beds' walls help keep soil and mulch from spilling onto paths, keeping your garden area neater. And fourth, raised beds are easy to protect from tunneling pests, such as moles and gophers, so you don't end up feeding your harvest to uninvited critters. Best of all, raised beds are an effective way to reclaim weedy spots where the soil has baked hard and nothing ever survives, no matter how much you amend the soil.

It is possible to grow any vegetable or herb, as well as flowers and berry bushes, in raised beds. I have planted raised-bed gardens ranging in size from twelve 4 x 8-foot beds (while also maintaining a fruit orchard) to two 2 x 4-foot beds. The size of your garden all depends on your available space and the amount of fresh produce you can consume on a regular basis.

Raised beds are generally made 3 to 4 feet wide. This width is a comfortable reach for most people and allows access to the center of the bed from both sides, so everything from transplanting to maintenance to harvesting is easy to deal with. The standard raised bed height is 12 inches. You can make higher beds, though I would advise putting a 6-inch layer of gravel at the bottom of beds that are higher than 2 feet. (This will help with drainage.) The length of the bed is up to you. I work with beds that are 4, 6, or 8 feet long; you could always extend that length, depending on your situation. Having a very long bed is fine, as long as it is not too wide or too narrow. Raised beds should never be narrower than 1 foot wide, so plant roots have room to spread out. Containers are sometimes smaller than that, based on the specific plants that will be grown in them. (See Chapter 6 for information on growing specific plants.)

If you are putting your raised bed on top of an existing lawn, put down a $\frac{1}{2}$-inch-thick layer of newspaper first, to prevent the turf from growing up through the bed. The beds can be placed directly on soil, lawn, or weeds (just trim them back as much as you can first), regardless of the condition of the earth. The only requirement is that the surface beneath the bed be porous.

You'll have to decide on the number of beds that will work in your available space, that you'll have time to care for, and that you'll be able to consume the harvest from. It's generally better to have a series of small beds rather than one giant bed; it's easier to maneuver around and maintain a small bed, and it makes crop rotation easier because you can plant in different beds each season. I predict that if you try the raised-bed system this year, next year you'll put in another bed—maybe one given over entirely to perennial wanderers, such as strawberries. (And if you do, you can companion-plant with borage to enhance the fruit's flavor and yield. Just plant a few borage plants in the corners of the bed, though, as it readily self-sows.)

The raised-bed kits I use are based on a 17th-century design using 1¼-inch-thick planks of Vermont white cedar. Because they are held together with mortise and tenon joints and a small wooden peg, they can be assembled and disassembled in a matter of minutes. (See the Farmstead entry in Resources on page 176.)

BUILDING RAISED BEDS

Raised beds can be simple mounds of soil or they can be more formal structures that enclose soil within a framework of wood, brick, concrete, or rock.

One great option for creating unframed raised beds is known as *lasagna gardening*, developed by Patricia Lanza. It's similar to sheet composting and is described in Chapter 4 (see page 24). This no-till option creates great soil and is quick and easy to do: Simply layer wet newspapers, peat moss, grass clippings, chopped leaves, and compost, and you have a raised bed.

Unframed beds make efficient use of limited or irregularly shaped spaces, such as along the foundation of a house. They're also more cost-effective than raised beds with solid sides. One of their few drawbacks is that in rainy climates, the soil in an unframed bed may eventually spread out; however, it's easy to add new soil to the bed and remound it from time to time.

Framed beds can be made out of any number of materials: untreated lumber, especially redwood or cedar, which are naturally rot-resistant; bricks; broken-up and stacked concrete; pavers; and rocks are all good options.

Framed raised beds help keep soil from washing away and create order in the garden. If you have a weedy patch with horribly unworkable soil—the kind of spot weeds love—plop a raised bed down on top of it. Your weed problem will vanish, and the soil underneath will begin its slow, much-needed recovery process.

It's not hard to build a framed raised bed. Here's how to install a 4-foot x 8-foot x 12-inch raised bed out of untreated lumber.

MATERIALS

4 posts, 4" x 4" x 12"

2 boards, 2" x 12" x 4'

2 boards, 2" x 12" x 8'

32 hot-dipped galvanized box nails

1 piece of heavy-gauge ¼" wire mesh, 4' x 8' (optional)

8 hot-dipped galvanized box nails for attaching wire mesh (optional)

The 12-inch posts will be used as blocking for constructing the raised bed, which will rest directly on the ground. Attach a post to each end of each 4-foot board. Anchor the board with a nail near its bottom edge, and then add nails every 3 inches. Repeat with the 8-foot boards, placing them perpendicular to the shorter boards to create an open rectangle. If gophers or moles are a problem in your yard, nail wire mesh to the bottom of the bed. Attach the mesh at each corner post and at the midpoint of each board.

FRAMED RAISED BED. It's easy to build a raised bed using untreated lumber, such as cedar or redwood.

CHOOSING THE RIGHT WOOD

Untreated woods are the way to go when creating your kitchen garden. Railroad ties and pressure-treated lumber contain harmful chemicals like creosote and arsenic, which can leach into your soil and subsequently into your vegetables. You can easily identify pressure-treated lumber by the hash marks on the side where the chemicals were injected into the wood. Always purchase untreated wood for gardening projects and especially for planters that will contain food crops.

Once the bed is constructed, simply place it on top of any porous surface and fill it with the soil mix I describe in Chapter 4. If you are placing your raised beds directly on top of your lawn, you will want to line the bottoms of the beds with a $\frac{1}{2}$-inch-thick layer of overlapping newspaper sheets before filling them with soil, to prevent the grass from growing up into the beds.

If you plan to water your garden with drip irrigation, I make the extra effort to bring in the water supply unobtrusively, which may mean via underground pipes. You should run any underground pipes at the same time as you are making your raised beds, either framed or unframed, rather than after your beds are filled with soil and plants.

CONTAINERS

Even the smallest patio, deck, or fire escape can be transformed into a kitchen garden, provided that it gets sufficient sun to grow vegetables and herbs. If your space is very limited, or if you simply want to limit the quantity of vegetables you grow in a season, containers are a great option. Most vegetables and herbs can be grown in pots, just as many fruits can be.

While herbs can be grown in 6-inch pots, the minimum size for vegetables is generally 10 inches, with a similar depth. (Several vegetables and fruit trees require deeper pots—a minimum of 18 inches.) Larger containers are better because they do not dry out as quickly and they allow for a variety of vegetables, herbs, and flowers to be planted together. When planting a large container, place it in its designated spot first, then fill it with soil and plants. It may be too heavy to move after it's planted.

I recommend sticking with the same type of material for all of your containers; this will give your garden a more polished look. If you'd like to introduce a little variety, use a mix of shapes and sizes of whatever type you choose.

Unglazed clay pots are porous, which allows air to circulate more easily to the root zone; the downside of this is that soil moisture evaporates more rapidly and you'll have to water more often. On a positive note, evaporation is a cooling process, and plants in unglazed clay pots have some summertime protection against ultrahot soil, which can burn roots. Glazed clay pots are less porous than unglazed pots, so evaporation is less of a problem. However, glazed pots are considerably more expensive than their unglazed counterparts. Both types of clay pots are best used in frost-free areas because they are prone to cracking in freezing temperatures.

Plastic pots are inexpensive, light, and practically unbreakable. They are nonporous, so they hold water well. But the soil in plastic pots can become very hot, especially in summer, and that can cause root burn. When choosing plastic pots, purchase light-color pots, rather than dark ones, and make sure they have drainage holes.

Hanging baskets are great for herbs, nasturtiums, and cherry tomatoes. Wire hanging baskets should be lined before planting; this will keep soil and plants in place. Coconut coir is an attractive liner for wire baskets, but it does tend to dry out quickly, so you will likely need to water your wire hanging baskets frequently.

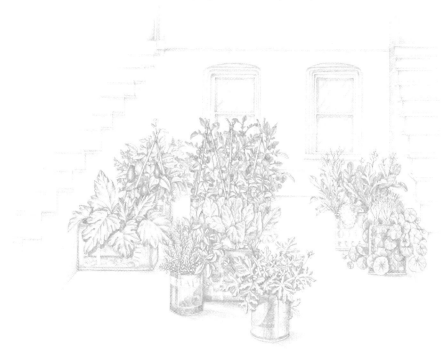

FOUND OBJECTS. Oil and vegetable tins add color and variety to the container garden.

Metal and concrete containers tend to be very heavy and are often expensive. Metal containers, in particular, can get hot enough to cook plants from the inside out. For that reason, it's best to use metal containers only in areas with some shade, to prevent overheating, and plant shade-tolerant crops like lettuces and certain herbs such as parsley and chervil.

Found objects (such as wooden wine boxes, whiskey barrels, and old drawers that have been stripped of any paint) can have a second life as planters, as can old bathtubs, wheelbarrows, and large vegetable or oil tins. However, I would caution against using abandoned truck tires and other recycled materials that may contain plastics, rubber, chemical residues, or petroleum, because they have the potential to leach harmful chemicals into your garden soil. Regardless of the found object, remember that you must drill or punch drainage holes in the bottom before planting. Unsealed wooden wine boxes, whiskey barrels, and drawers should also be sealed with Danish oil before planting.

Recycled pots and found objects must be scrubbed and cleaned before you plant in them. This will keep any soilborne viruses and other diseases of previous plant inhabitants from being passed on.

· 4 ·

CREATING AMAZING SOIL

The key to successful organic gardening is good soil.

Without good soil to grow and live in, your vegetables will not perform. It doesn't matter if you have sun, water, and good seeds or transplants to work with if the soil in your kitchen garden is not nutrient-rich.

I put in a garden for some friends who insisted that their location was unsuitable for growing vegetables. For 10 years, their garden never provided produce they could use. I put in a raised bed on top of their soil, and now they have a bumper crop. Their plants are growing like gangbusters because it is actually a perfect spot—a sunny plot on the top of a hill. They had the sun and easy access for watering and maintenance. What they didn't have was the soil—which is the most important thing.

If you use compost to amend soil in the ground, it can take years before your soil is rich and friable over the long haul. This is why I like growing in raised beds—there's no lengthy time commitment. You can see the results of using excellent soil immediately.

I happened upon the soil used in my raised beds quite by accident when I was setting up my garden in Mt. Washington. The earth was clay backfill, behind a retaining wall, so growing in the ground was not an option. It was so compacted that a grown man literally could not put a shovel in it to turn it over. Because of this, I knew I had to grow aboveground, in a raised bed. A gardener friend told me about Tim, a man in Altadena who had the best soil she'd ever worked with—it wasn't actually soil at all, but rather stable bedding made up of composted horse manure, wood shavings, and straw.

Though I was rather skeptical that this would be a suitable growing medium, I nevertheless ordered some, filled my raised beds with it, amended it with bonemeal and greensand, and then started my plants. I soon realized that this light, fluffy, nutrient-rich "soil" was the best medium to grow in. In 2 weeks, my plants literally took off. Because I saw results so quickly, I became an immediate convert. There was much more leaf development than normal because the mixture was so rich in nitrogen. And I loved that it was so simple and easy. No bagged soil, no complicated assortment of amendments needed. Most important, I was working with a soil that was alive—it was full of worms, bacteria, fungi, and other microbes.

I never till my soil, stir it up, or compact it down, and I really only disturb it when I add amendments. Each season it compacts a bit on its own, so I top it off with another layer of compost from my own bins that I've amended with bonemeal and greensand. I follow this pattern throughout the year, adding more layers at the start of each growing season.

My beds mimic the mulched humus floor of a forest where plant residue, green and brown, thick and thin, is laid down over centuries without ever being stirred, tilled, or compacted. It is rich in a spectrum of nutrients, the combined contributions of a diverse assortment of species, animal and vegetable, some still living and many more long dead. Below the surface, microbes and fungi work away at the decay while insects aerate the soil. It's a moist environment, spongelike both in texture and absorbency.

MANURE IN THE GARDEN

I have to stress that the mix that I'm using contains well-composted horse manure, not raw horse manure full of weed seeds and harmful bacteria. You may be reluctant to eat vegetables grown entirely in manure, but I can assure you that the fermentation that takes place during the composting process eliminates the impurities and bacteria that you associate with fresh manure. Furthermore, fresh manure gets very hot and stays that way for at least 2 weeks as it is composting down, so I do not recommend putting it directly in the garden, as it can burn plant roots and seeds. When checking out a new source of manure and picking up a load, you should be able to put your hand in the pile and not be burned. If you can do that, you'll know that it has fully composted and is safe from both heat and germ standpoints.

Animal manure contains a vast amount of plant nutrition, and that's what makes it a key component of the French intensive planting method. Plants grown in nutrient-rich manure can be placed closer together than those planted in ordinary soil, making it possible to produce three times the quantity of produce in the same amount of space. In the late 1800s and early 1900s, intensive market gardeners developed an efficient gardening system around New York and Philadelphia. The fertility of their plots depended on an

NOT ALL MANURES ARE THE SAME

The beneficial qualities of manure for vegetative growth have been known for millennia—literally since the dawn of agriculture. The word itself, "manure," comes from a Middle English verb meaning "to cultivate land."

While all animal manures are good sources of nutrients for plants, not all manures are the same. Rabbit manure provides the most nitrogen of any manure, so if you are using it in quantity, compensate with an additional high-carbon ingredient (such as sawdust or shredded paper). Chicken manure is second only to rabbit manure in terms of the amount of nitrogen it delivers to the soil. Thanks to a recent trend that has popularized urban poultry raising, chicken manure is no longer an expensive packaged additive only found at nurseries. You may be able to get it from your neighbors. Horse, cow, duck, and sheep manures all provide roughly the same rate of nitrogen, which is half that of chicken manure.

However, don't use dog or cat manure in your gardens, as it may contain disease organisms harmful to humans. Toss pet waste in the garbage.

abundance of organic matter, most in the form of horse manure, which meant that an active manure trade existed throughout the 19th century in both cities.

You may wonder about the availability of horse manure near you. Even if you're deep in the heart of the city, I'd wager that there are horses—and horse manure—closer than you think. Ask around, call the local riding stable, consult the growers and vendors at your farmers' market. Getting it to your garden might take a little effort, like borrowing a pickup truck, or you may find that it's easy to find someone willing to drop off a few wheelbarrows of composted manure to your site.

GROWING IN RAISED BEDS, *NOT* IN GROUND

As described in Chapter 3, my *Homegrown* method of intensive planting involves growing in raised beds and containers, which allows you to easily control the soil mix so it remains loose and fertile. Few of us are lucky enough to already have well-aerated garden soil that is rich in organic matter. While it is possible to improve your existing soil through the regular addition of organic material, especially compost, it can be a very long-term undertaking, depending on the relative health of your soil.

If you fill your framed raised beds with a mix of stable bedding, bonemeal, and greensand, you will be able to harvest vegetables, flowers, and herbs within a single season. For my beds, I mix 10 pounds each of bonemeal and greensand per 100 square feet of stable bedding.

If you do not have access to stable bedding, the lasagna gardening method is another option for creating amazing soil. You can use it either in framed or unframed raised beds.

To make a lasagna garden, first cut any existing grass or weeds as short as possible, and then place your raised bed frame, if you're using one, directly on the ground; you can use string to mark out the areas to be planted in unframed raised beds. Remember, a series of smaller raised beds no wider than 3 to 4 feet across is preferable to one giant bed. Next, cover the bed with a $\frac{1}{2}$-inch-thick layer of overlapping newspaper sheets to kill off any existing vegetation. On top of the newspaper, layer compost or composted manure (you should have already dusted this with bonemeal and greensand), leaves, shredded paper, grass clippings, organic kitchen scraps, and coffee grounds that you have dusted with bonemeal and greensand. Finish with a 3- to 4-inch-thick layer of soil or well-finished compost. You want a good variety of materials in your lasagna layers because that will supply your garden with a good variety of nutrients. Keep layering until the finished bed is at least 1 foot deep.

Once all of the layers are in place, water the soil and then let it sit for 2 weeks before planting in it. By no means will it be fully decomposed after 2 weeks—it will have started

---

ROCK POWDERS TO IMPROVE YOUR SOIL

Organic farmer Eliot Coleman suggests amending your soil with mineral supplements in the form of rock powders to replace the minerals removed from your soil in the form of harvested crops.

Phosphate rock and bonemeal are both good sources of phosphorus. Phosphorus promotes good flower and fruit production, and it is the nutrient most likely to be deficient in your garden soil.

Greensand is a slow-release source of potassium and trace elements. Potassium is an important nutrient for good root development, plant health, and vigor.

Initially, you should apply phosphate rock and greensand directly on the garden soil at a rate of 10 pounds each per 100 square feet. Lightly till the amendments into the surface of the soil to a depth of no more than 2 inches, then water after lightly tilling. After that, it's easier and more effective to sprinkle these products very lightly on the green layer of your compost pile.

LASAGNA GARDENING. This quick no-till option creates great soil and can provide a more efficient use of limited space than a raised bed with solid sides.

to break down, but you may still see uncomposted clumps, shreds of newspapers, or kitchen scraps, and that's fine. You want texture like that in your soil mix to keep it loose and fluffy. If you plan to toss in hard or fibrous kitchen scraps (like melon rinds and onion skins), cut them into smaller pieces to speed up the composting process.

The best compost is made from the best ingredients, so try to use only organic scraps, especially in this quick-and-dirty soil. If you use nonorganic materials, there's the possibility of pesticide residue.

SOIL FOR CONTAINER GARDENS

The key to growing vegetables in containers is growing in a soil mix that is very light and not easily compacted. Using soil from your yard in your containers is not a good idea. Even if it is nutrient-rich and well balanced, the very structure of garden soil presents problems for container gardens. The main problems are that garden soil is heavy, so it will not drain well, and it will compact, which means roots will not get enough oxygen for growth.

The soil blend I fill my pots with is one-third high-quality organic potting soil, one-third peat moss, and one-third compost or composted manure. I further amend this mix with bonemeal and greensand.

SOIL TESTING

Maintaining a healthy, living soil is crucial to organic gardening. And while regularly applying organic material to your soil will help keep your soil alive, all soils are different and they do not all respond equally to applications of minerals or compost.

In order to be certain of any mineral deficiencies, you can have your soil tested by a soil-testing laboratory. Contact your local Cooperative Extension Service for a soil test kit. (Nutrient deficiencies may also be observed through your plants themselves; see Chapter 8 for common symptoms.)

It is also important to monitor your soil's pH. Most garden vegetables thrive at a pH of 6 to 7 (slightly acidic). You can determine your soil's pH by purchasing a testing kit from a garden supply catalog or a good nursery. If your soil is too acidic (below 6), add limestone by sprinkling it on the soil and mixing it in. If your soil is too alkaline (above 7), add acidic organic matter, such as peat moss, and lightly till it into the soil to a depth of no more than 2 inches. Water lightly.

If you do not have access to compost or composted manure, you can mix chopped raw organic vegetable scraps directly into your potting soil mix, though you should wait 2 weeks before planting in it to allow the raw materials time to begin breaking down.

WHY COMPOST AFTER YOU'VE MADE A RAISED BED?

Compost is the end result of the decomposition of organic matter, and it is a natural, slow-release fertilizer. By adding compost to your soil, you provide your plants with the micronutrients they need to succeed. Once your garden is up and running, you will have such a great quantity of plant material from your beds, especially at the end of a season, that composting will begin to make sense. Rather than dump your vegetable scraps in your town's "green" recycling bin or—even worse—in the trash, you can easily recycle them yourself by using them again in your garden. (You will want to dispose of any diseased plants in the trash, though.) You are going to be generating a huge amount of compostable material, and there is no reason to just give that away. You know what these plants' lives were like—they were free of chemical fertilizers, pesticides, and diseases. You can't buy that at the nursery.

COMPOSTING THROUGH HISTORY

The first written mention of compost in agriculture is found on Mesopotamian clay tablets dating from approximately 2300 BC. Around 2,000 years later, the first book written in prose Latin came out: Cato the Elder's *De Agricultura,* a plainspoken how-to manual on successfully and economically setting up and maintaining a farm.

Cato's composting directions are for the two-bin method. One bin (or pit, in his case) was for finished, ready-to-use compost, while the second was for material not yet composted down. To get material ready for the pit, all compostable greens and browns were scattered in stables and corrals. Cattle and horses would trample the waste, smashing it into smaller pieces and drenching it with their urine (liquid manure). From there, the refuse was put into the pit, where it would get turned regularly for a year. Letting compost rest in the pits before applying it was essential, according to Cato; this was one of his "revolutionary" approaches to agriculture.

Composting was an important though often unheralded practice that propped up more than a few of the great civilizations. Cleopatra deified the earthworm, and mentions of composting appear in the Bhagavad Gita, the Talmud, and the Bible, as well as in the writings of Shakespeare, Sir Francis Bacon, Thomas Jefferson, and George Washington.

Modern composting was pioneered by Sir Albert Howard, father of organic gardening and creator of the Indore method, which was named after the town in India where he lived in the early 20th century. Howard promoted a layering system, in which plant materials and manure are stacked in piles that are then watered well and turned twice, at 6 weeks and 12 weeks.

I have read stories about people taking their compost piles with them when they move, and I completely understand. When you see what compost can do for you and your garden, you'll get attached to yours, too! And in some places, composting, like recycling in general, has gone from being a lifestyle choice people make on a personal level to a policy mandated by legislators. In the summer of 2009, San Francisco enacted a law that all residents and businesses must participate in the municipal composting program, which was already the most ambitious in the country. Nearly two-thirds of the organic garbage that San Franciscans send to landfills—almost 500,000 tons annually—could be composted, and the new law is an effort to make composting as common as separating bottles, paper, and cans for recycling. Nationwide, according to the EPA, only 2.2 percent of the 31.1 million tons of food waste created in 2005 was diverted from landfills to composting.

Besides being very beneficial to plants, composting is also good for the environment. It reduces the need for petroleum-based fertilizers and lessens water use, since compost-rich soil is more absorbent, thanks to having a greater proportion of organic material. It has been said that composting is the single most important task an organic gardener or farmer can perform, and I have to agree. Compost creates healthy soil, which in turn supports strong plants with fewer disease and pest problems. That's nature's way.

COMPOSTING MADE EASY

There are a variety of ways to produce great compost; choosing the best method for you depends on the amount of space you have for compost, the amount of time and effort you are willing to put into making compost, and the amount of compost you need for your garden. For home gardeners, I recommend any of the following three methods.

Two-Bin Composting

For gardeners with sufficient outdoor space to accommodate two compost bins, I have found the two-bin system to be the ideal way to build your own royal soil for future use in your beds. When properly built and maintained, this hot composting method can create compost that is ready to use in roughly 8 weeks.

Your first consideration with the two-bin system is the type of container to use. There are many designs for composting bins: boxes made of wire mesh, wood slats, and wood frames; plastic snap-together boxes; plastic bell-shaped domes; tumblers; perforated barrels and garbage cans; cement block or straw bale enclosures; lengths of snow fence shaped into cylinders; and three-walled trenches.

In colder or dry climates, as well as in urban areas, you'll want to select containers with few, if any, openings on the sides or top in order to keep your compost hot, moist, and pest-free. In humid climates, containers with multiple openings on the sides are a good option because they regulate your compost temperature and moisture levels.

Regardless of the type of bins you are using, each one must hold a minimum of 1 cubic yard of material in order to create good compost (a 3 x 3 x 3-foot cube holds 1 cubic yard of material). The ideal site for your compost bins is a shady spot close to the kitchen, close to the garden, close to water, and easy to work around.

TWO-BIN COMPOSTING. Having two compost piles going at once will provide you with finished compost throughout the year. A two-bin system allows you to build your first pile all at once to begin hot composting, while the second bin allows you to add green and brown materials over time.

The two-bin method requires you to fill one bin all at once, while you fill the second bin gradually over time. This provides you with a receptacle for your kitchen and yard wastes while you simultaneously produce compost in your first bin.

To fill your compost bins, begin with a 3-inch layer of brown material, preferably straw. Add 1 to 6 inches of green material, then a 1-inch layer of soil or well-finished compost that has been lightly dusted with bonemeal and greensand, and then another 3-inch layer of brown material. Continue layering in this manner until the pile reaches a minimum of 36 inches tall, and top with a layer of brown material. The thickness of the green layers will depend on the materials used. Bulky material such as plant stems can

GREEN AND BROWN

When collecting materials for your compost, you will want to seek out both high-nitrogen green items and high-carbon brown items. Mix together a broad range of materials with different mineral makeups to get finished compost that contains every nutrient on the spectrum.

Common green materials include: garden plants, weeds, grass clippings, seaweed, fruit and vegetable scraps, eggshells, crustacean shells, peanut shells, coffee grounds, tea leaves, hair, and manure.

Common brown materials include: fallen leaves, shredded newspaper and cardboard, lint, wood chips, and straw.

WHAT *NOT* TO COMPOST

There are some materials that shouldn't be added to the compost pile. They include: pet waste from dogs, cats, and birds, as they may carry organisms that are parasitic to humans; any meat or bone scraps; chemically treated wood; dairy products such as cheese or butter; oil-based foods such as mayonnaise, dressings, and peanut butter; diseased plants; and plants, fruits, and vegetables that have been sprayed with synthetic pesticides. Send them to the landfill, instead.

Leaf litter from eucalyptus, bamboo, and avocado take a long time to break down and should be avoided. Large amounts of highly acid materials, such as pine needles and oak leaves, should also be used sparingly, unless you are creating compost for acid-loving crops such as blueberries.

---

be applied in a thicker layer, whereas dense material such as kitchen scraps or grass clippings should be layered more thinly. The thin layers of soil or well-finished compost throughout the pile will activate the composting process, as they contain millions of beneficial microorganisms.

The compost pile should remain slightly moist at all times, like a squeezed-out sponge, as the beneficial bacteria within it thrive in moist conditions. Compost also requires air. Using a sturdy stick, pitchfork, or specially designed compost-turning tool or aerator, stir the materials in your bins every few days to make air available throughout the pile.

If the materials in your first bin are consistently moist and well aerated, they will heat up considerably as they begin to compost down. Once the pile cools (in approximately 8 weeks), even though it's not fully broken down, the compost will be ready for use in your garden.

Common problems with hot composting include odor and a pile's failure to heat up. A well-made compost pile is odorless. When the pile is too wet or too compacted, the process becomes anaerobic (without air) and very foul-smelling. The solution to this is to aerate and add more brown material to the pile. The best way to do this is to remove all of the existing (smelly) compost from the bin and start the layering process over again, using the existing compost for the green layers and adding plenty of brown materials in between.

If your pile fails to heat up, it may be because it is too dry. This is easily remedied by turning the pile and watering it with a hose or a watering can. Another reason the heap may fail to heat up is an excess of brown material and not enough green material. A quick

THE THREE STAGES OF COMPOST. Compost has a number of stages of readiness. Compost can be ready to use in a few weeks, if it's heated enough to break down most materials. Let it cool and work it into your soil to amend your raised beds and containers. You may still be able to distinguish some of the original materials in this first stage of compost, but it will continue to break down in the soil. For more thoroughly decomposed compost, heat up your pile a second time by adding a diluted liquid fertilizer such as fish emulsion with kelp and aerating it. After it heats up and cools down for a second time, you won't be able to distinguish any of the original compost materials because it will be dark and crumbly; use second-stage compost to enrich your soil and add nutrients. Third-stage compost is well-finished compost that's been heated up and cooled two times and aged for 1 to 2 years. At this point, the compost has a chocolate fudge cake texture throughout and supports beneficial microorganisms to improve soil quality.

remedy for this situation is to add a high-nitrogen liquid organic fertilizer (such as fish emulsion with kelp) to the pile. You will want to dissolve the liquid fertilizer in water before adding it to the pile (follow the instructions on the label). If this fails to stimulate the bacteria in the pile (you should see results in a couple of days), you should then start the pile over, using the existing (cold) compost for the brown layers and adding plenty of green materials in between.

Composting Directly in the Garden

For gardeners who do not have the space or time to maintain a two-bin composting system, it is possible to compost directly in the garden. This involves less work than bin composting, but it takes longer for the compost to be finished—anywhere from 6 months to 2 years.

One such cold composting method is known as "sheet composting."

Sheet composting simply involves spreading a thin layer of raw organic materials on top of your existing soil and allowing earthworms to break those materials down. In order to avoid anaerobic conditions or unpleasant smells, it is important that you carefully balance your green and brown materials. The base layer of your sheet compost should consist of green materials, while the top layer should be made up of brown materials (straw and shredded leaves work especially well). Once the materials in your compost layer have begun to break down, the bed is ready for planting.

Another way to compost directly in the garden and get rid of kitchen scraps is known as "kitchen blender compost." Just place your raw, organic kitchen waste, including eggshells and coffee grounds, in your blender, add enough water to cover the scraps, and blend until finely chopped. Pour this liquid compost into trenches dug in your beds, and cover it with soil. Once the liquid compost is absorbed into the surrounding soil, the beds will be ready for planting. (You can also add blender compost to a compost pile as a green layer.)

Both methods for composting directly in the garden are great for gardeners in cold climates, as compost materials can be applied at the end of the main growing season and allowed to break down over the winter.

Worm Bins

For apartment-dwellers with no yard available for a two-bin system, composting can also be done (on a more limited scale) on a fire escape, under the kitchen sink, on a balcony, in a garage, or in a basement. A worm bin allows you to turn raw organic food waste into compost very easily. Admittedly, you can't do this if you're squeamish about worms or the notion that you have worms residing in close proximity, and you must be willing to care for the worms properly. It's not hard work, but it does require your attention.

It is possible to buy a ready-made worm bin, or you can make one yourself. You will need a container with 1 square foot of surface area for each pound of worms and kitchen scraps.

If you're making your own, plastic storage bins or wooden boxes with lids are both good options, as long as what you choose is at least 12 inches deep. You will want to drill a minimum of ten $\frac{1}{4}$-inch holes in the lid and around the top of the sides of the bin for air circulation.

Your worms will require about 8 inches of bedding material, such as leaves, potting soil, or 1-inch-wide strips of newspaper. It is important to keep the bedding material moist. (You can use a plant mister to occasionally moisten it.)

Once your bedding is in place, add your worms, which are available for sale on the Internet and at many nurseries and farmers' markets. You will want to add red wiggler worms (*Eisenia fetida* or *Lumbricus rubellus*) to your bin, not earthworms taken from your garden. Cover your worms with a thin layer of moistened, shredded newspaper before adding kitchen scraps.

Start by feeding your worms slowly. More than 1 pound of food per pound of worms will go uneaten, begin to rot, and attract flies. After a week or two, your worms will have adjusted to their new home and will begin to efficiently process your kitchen scraps.

The best materials to add to a worm bin are raw, organic fruit and vegetable scraps; coffee grounds and filters; tea leaves; eggshells; paper napkins and towels; and dead plants and flowers. Remember to feed worms a varied diet and don't overload the bin with fruit, or you'll attract fruit flies. Do not feed your worms meat, fish, or dairy products. After adding food to your worm bin, you will want to cover it with a thin layer of moistened, shredded newspaper. Red wrigglers are most active when temperatures range between 60° and 80°F. They become more sluggish and eat less when the temperature falls out of this range.

When the bedding starts to resemble dark, crumbly soil (usually in 1 to 4 months), it's time to harvest your compost. Move all of the bedding that resembles soil over to one side of the worm bin. Add new, damp bedding to the empty side, and start placing food scraps on that side. In about a month, most of the worms should move over to the new bedding, allowing you to scoop out the relatively worm-free compost left behind.

USING COMPOST

While fully broken down or well-finished compost can be used throughout the garden at any time of the year, half-finished compost is best applied at the end of the main growing season so that by spring it will have completed its decomposition.

Regardless of how fully broken down your compost is, you will want to spread it on top of the soil and mix it in shallowly, just 1 to 2 inches down. You'll have superior plant growth if you try to duplicate nature's system of leaving organic matter on the surface to be mixed in by earthworms. To maintain your soil's health, I recommend adding a 1-inch layer of compost to the surface of your soil and then mixing it in shallowly at the start of each growing season.

In order for your vegetables, flowers, and herbs to thrive, I further recommend using well-finished compost as a side-dressing for your plants throughout the season. Simply scatter some well-finished compost on the surface of the soil around the bases of your plants, and water it in.

Compost tea is also a great fertilizer for your plants. It's very easy to make small batches of compost tea: Just place a cloth bag filled with well-finished compost in your watering can, and add water. You will want to use 1 pound of well-finished compost per gallon of water. Stir for a couple of minutes, and let it sit overnight. Your compost tea is now ready for use in your gardens and containers.

· 5 ·

SEEDS, SEEDLINGS, AND PLANTING

Several years ago I paid a visit to Monticello, Thomas Jefferson's home in Virginia, both to look at the architecture and to tour the famous gardens. I came back with souvenirs—seeds of more than 50 different varieties of vegetables and flowers. I loved their connection to our American history and, in a larger sense, to world history. Jefferson's intention was not only to grow food to eat, but also to collect seeds from all over the world to build a patrimonial seed bank.

I still grow arugula directly descended from the seeds I bought at Monticello—garden rocket, an easy-to-grow, spicy-yet-nutty, open-pollinated green that Jefferson himself probably ate. I've been collecting the seeds ever since I planted my first batch, saving them both for next year's garden and for gifts for friends. It's that special. A few years ago, I stumbled across an 1869 European heirloom, 'Perpetual Spinach', that is amazingly heat-tolerant. One of my plants produced for 2½ years, through many heat waves. This heirloom is technically a chard, but it tastes and cooks exactly like spinach. Part of my initial inspiration in writing *Homegrown* was to introduce people not only to the pleasures of fresh homegrown food but also to unusual varieties of vegetables like this chard.

A kitchen garden planted with a wide variety of vegetables, flowers, and herbs is not only a more natural garden, but it is also an inspiration for the home cook or chef. The mix of shapes, sizes, and colors in my garden regularly inspires me to try new combinations of ingredients. A simple salad of mixed lettuces is even better with homegrown arugula flowers, Florence fennel fronds, and marjoram. When my meals are as beautiful as the garden that provided the raw materials, I know I have succeeded in the kitchen.

DIVERSITY IN THE GARDEN

As Sally Jean Cunningham notes in her book *Great Garden Companions,* ". . . we can make a difference by planning gardens and landscapes that won't need chemicals to keep them looking good. And a very good way to start is by creating a more diverse environment in your own yard and garden. Almost any combination of plants grown together is better than segregating crops into separate blocks."

Interplanting vegetables, herbs, and flowers is a very old gardening concept; it encourages biodiversity, while planting a single uniform monocrop does not. If you have one bed full of the exact same type of plant and you have an insect or fungal problem, the entire bed may be lost. By interplanting flowers and herbs among your vegetables, you will attract natural predators, such as birds and beneficial insects, and make it harder for pest insects to find the crop they prefer.

Again, look to nature. In wild areas, we do not have swaths of one thing. When we do, it's usually because something invasive has been introduced. My best local example of this is Griffith Park, more than 4,000 acres of undeveloped land in the heart of Los Angeles. This park is quickly becoming covered in wild mustard, a fast-growing bush that is threatening to turn the diverse natural chaparral into a monoculture of this invasive species.

I have had clients tell me that they don't want to "waste space" on something they won't eat. I had a client who insisted on growing nothing but bell peppers and tomatoes. I feared it would be a disaster, and I said so. The result was that she had nothing but pests all season long because there were only two kinds of plants in her large garden, which is not enough diversity to build a healthy ecosystem.

INTENSIVE PLANTING METHOD

Intensive planting offers one huge benefit: A large number of plants can be grown in a very small space—up to three times the quantity grown in a conventional garden that's planted in rows. I first became interested in this method when I knew I was moving to Los Angeles and realized that I would probably have a small garden. This method seemed to make the most sense. Crowding plants has never seemed strange to me because that's how they grow in the wild.

Just as nature is your guide in terms of plant diversity, it is also your guide in terms of plant density in an intensively planted garden. A natural landscape is not organized into tidy rows of well-spaced plants. Rather, many different types of plants grow immediately adjacent to one another. In an intensively planted garden, plants are placed close together over the entire bed, rather than in rows, so that their leaves overlap at maturity. This continuous leafy canopy means little to no soil surface is exposed, cutting down on evaporation and weeds.

COMPANION PLANTING

Companion planting also plays a role in the intensive planting method, as vegetables, flowers, and herbs are crowded together. It is important that plants known to grow well

---

VEGETABLE FAMILIES AND COMMON HERB AND FLOWER COMPANIONS

Beet Family: Beets, spinach, and Swiss chard. **Friends:** Borage, chives, Florence fennel, garlic, lavender, and shallots.

Cabbage Family: Arugula, broccoli rabe, Brussels sprouts, cabbage, cauliflower, collards, horseradish, kale, mustard, radishes, and turnips. **Friends:** Rosemary, sage, and thyme.

Carrot Family: Carrots, celery, Florence fennel, and parsnips. **Friends:** Chives, rosemary, and sage.

Legume Family: Beans and peas. **Friends:** Basil, dill, savory, and tarragon.

Lettuce Family: Artichokes, endive, lettuce, and radicchio. **Friends:** Chives, garlic, leeks, and violets.

Onion Family: Asparagus, garlic, leeks, onions, and shallots. **Friends:** Cilantro, dill, and parsley.

Squash Family: Cucumbers, melons, pumpkins, and summer and winter squash. **Friends:** Borage, dill, and nasturtiums.

Tomato Family: Eggplant, peppers, potatoes, and tomatoes. **Friends:** Basil, calendula, and parsley.

together be planted near one another. This style of home gardening has been around for as long as people have grown food close to the kitchen. Its modern roots go back to the Elizabethan cottage garden and the French *potager*. However, before either the English or the French adopted these methods, the Three Sisters—corn, beans, and squash, the iconic perfect triangle of symbiotic companionship—were grown in America. Native Americans planted corn in groups of three or four, sowed winter squash and pumpkins around the corn, and planted pole beans at the base of the corn.

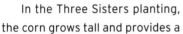
VARY YOUR PLANT HEIGHTS. For easy access and a beautiful layered look, place shorter plants in front of taller ones.

In the Three Sisters planting, the corn grows tall and provides a natural trellis for the beans to climb up. The squash covers the ground, thereby shading and cooling the soil. Squash is also prickly, so it keeps predators, especially mice, from eating the corn. The beans fix nitrogen in the soil for everybody.

If you plant the sisters in your *Homegrown*-style garden, add oregano and a sprig of *epazote* (a Mexican herb), and you have the makings of a nice soup.

Companionability appears in various forms and is beneficial for various reasons. Sometimes companion plantings provide a structure for other plants to climb, and sometimes companion plantings produce foot-wide leaves, like you'll find with squash, that shade everything below. Think about height when you're companion planting. If you want to grow lettuces in the summer, for example, put your taller companion plants to the south to create shade. On the other hand, if you're growing sun-loving veggies, put the climbers at the north end of the bed.

In a bed with melons and squash, both vining plants, I fill in the empty places with nasturtiums—lots of them. This makes a nice layered and heaped effect, with large, green, leafy vines snaking around delicate, pastel-colored flowers. If you are short on space in your raised bed, plant the melons, squash, and other vines near the edges of the bed, and let these wanderers spill out into the yard or grow up a trellis or fence.

GOOD COMPANIONS. Plant members of the same family near each other and fill in the spaces between them with their flower and herb companions.

When you're designing the plantings for each bed, it's important to manage heights and make sure that all of the soil surfaces are covered with a good mix of vegetables, flowers, and herbs. Plant vegetables of the same family near one another in the garden to make crop rotation easy to manage from season to season. (For more on crop rotation, see Chapter 8.)

SEEDS VERSUS TRANSPLANTS

While there are several advantages to growing from seed (including price and access to a wider variety of vegetables, flowers, and herbs than is typically found at the nursery or farmers' market), I nevertheless advise first-time gardeners to start with transplants in order to achieve better results in a shorter amount of time. Rather than risk having your seeds fail to germinate the first time you start a kitchen garden, you can improve your chances of success by using transplants from a local grower. Granted, if you are growing strictly from transplants, it is going to be more expensive than growing from seed. However, growing from transplants is cheaper than buying $5-a-pound heirloom tomatoes at the farmers' market. You do the math. Each transplant produces a huge amount of fruit. So is it affordable? Yes! You have an initial outlay of material costs for a raised-bed garden, but once it's established, your only yearly expenses are transplants (or seeds, eventually) and additional compost to have a season-long harvest of delicious heirloom tomatoes.

When choosing transplants of any kind, select healthy plants in 4-inch pots. You want plants that are short and compact rather than tall and lanky. Turn the plant over. If there are roots growing out of the bottom of the container, that's a sign that the plant is root-bound and may not grow well once transplanted. If you are buying a plant for its flowers, it helps if one bud is open so that you can see the actual color, but, in general, look for a mass of buds rather than a mass of blossoms.

Inspect all transplants for insects and their eggs. Check the undersides of leaves as well as the bottoms of containers, two favorite congregating places of insects.

Sometimes you have to sow seed, because not all vegetables transplant well. Vegetables that even first-time gardeners should not transplant include root crops such as beets, carrots, and radishes. Greens such as arugula, lettuce, and spinach germinate very quickly when directly sown in the garden, and transplanting is an unnecessary first step. Likewise, beans and peas should always be directly sown in the garden. I don't usually start slow-growing perennial vegetables and herbs, such as asparagus and rosemary, from seed. Because they can take several years to develop into full-size plants, I like to give them as much of a head start as possible.

After one or two seasons of growing in the garden, you will have a much better understanding of which plants work well in your microclimate and which plants you truly enjoy having access to on a daily basis. With a little experience under your belt, you'll be ready to start growing some of them from seed.

SEED AND VARIETY SELECTION

If you are going to start from seed, you have to first assess your commitment and then plan ahead. You will need a small amount of space near a sunny window or in a sunny outdoor spot in mild climates to devote to this process. This space is where you will place seed trays or small pots so you can monitor them every day to make sure that they don't dry out. It's not a difficult process, nor is it rocket science, but it does require a certain amount of care and attention.

If seed-starting is for you, let me welcome you to a beautifully complex world of diversity, both in your garden and on your plate. It is rare to find a local nursery with the selection of vegetables you can find in a single seed catalog, let alone a whole handful of heirloom and specialty catalogs. So if you would love to grow some more unusual cooking ingredients—say the vast array of chicories or shell beans—and eat them fresh from your garden, you'll need to put seed-starting on your to-do list.

Besides the incredible variety of flavors you get when growing from seed, you get the additional significant benefit of eliminating the threat of grower- or nursery-originated pests. If you are using transplants purchased from a garden center or nursery, it is very difficult to avoid bringing pests home with the plants.

The summer of 2009 was unusually wet and humid along the entire East Coast of the country. This resulted in a late blight that arrived atypically early, attacking tomato plants everywhere from the Southeast to Northeast, hitting front- and backyard gardens and commercial farms alike. According to plant pathologists, the source of the outbreak was industrial breeding operations that sold their stock to the large retail stores—exactly where many home gardeners get their plants. Perhaps the late blight outbreak was inevitable, due to the perfect storm of conditions, but it also brought home the message that starting from seed, or buying from a trusted local grower, can be more cost-efficient and worthwhile in the long run than using cheap, readily available transplants priced for the mass market.

The theory is simple enough: High-quality plants come from high-quality seeds. It is important to select varieties that are adapted to your area and that provide the size, color, and growth habit that's right for your garden and your taste buds. There are a number of vegetables, including cucumbers, eggplants, and tomatoes, that have been developed to grow on plants half the size of regular ones, making them good choices for growing in containers.

As you start shopping for seeds, it's important to know that seeds are either hybrid or open-pollinated. Hybrid seeds may be resistant to specific diseases and are guaranteed to have the desirable traits (such as higher yields) of the specific parent plants from which they were bred. The seed harvested from hybrid plants, however, will not produce another generation of plants exactly like the parent plants. In other words, if you want to grow that hybrid plant again, you'll have to purchase seeds each year, as hybrid plants do not breed true.

Open-pollinated seeds are the result of open pollination by insects or wind, and they typically produce plants very much like the parent plants, though there is the possibility of slight variations. (Variations between parent and offspring are more common in cross-pollinated plants like cucumbers and squash because it is difficult to control what the plants are openly cross-pollinated with, in contrast with self-pollinated plants like beans and tomatoes, which only pollinate themselves.) Heirloom varieties of vegetables, flowers, and herbs come from open-pollinated seeds, and they typically have a more pleasing taste and texture than hybrid varieties do. Plants grown from heirloom seeds are also likely to adapt to your local conditions over time, and heirloom varieties represent a vast pool of genetic characteristics that help to preserve diversity in the kitchen garden.

There are three main sources for seeds: local nurseries and hardware stores, mail-order catalogs, and seed exchanges. I recommend looking at a variety of mail-order catalogs, which provide a much wider selection of vegetables, flowers, and herbs than you'll be able to find at your local nursery or hardware store. There are also regional seed catalogs that specialize in varieties adapted to particular parts of the country, each with its own diverse climate. Organizations such as Seed Savers Exchange specialize in creating seed banks of heirloom varieties and facilitate seed exchanges between their members. For a list of specialty seed providers, see Resources on page 175.

READING SEED PACKETS

While some seeds keep for several years if stored properly, I advise you to purchase only enough seed for the current year's use. The label on the seed packet will note the year for which the seeds were packaged, and the seeds should not be used if they are more than 1 or 2 years old.

Hybrid seeds will be identified as such, either by use of the word "hybrid" or "F1" in parentheses following the name. (F1 hybrids are the first generation of a controlled cross-pollination between two parent plants.) The label will also indicate if the seeds were treated with a synthetic chemical fungicide. This kind of seed treatment sterilizes the soil immediately surrounding the seed, which has the potential, especially with repeated use, to diminish the overall health of your garden soil. I only use untreated seeds in my organic kitchen garden.

Disease resistance, if it exists, will be mentioned on the seed label. It is especially common to find varieties of tomatoes that are resistant to fusarium and verticillium wilt, and sometimes even to nematodes and tobacco mosaic virus, as well. In order to help maintain the overall health of my kitchen garden, I seek out disease-resistant varieties whenever possible.

Seed packets will also indicate when and how to sow the seeds, the best growing conditions for the plant, and the number of days, on average, to germination and harvest.

REGIONAL PLANTING TIMES

Planting times will differ by growing season and regional weather conditions. Most of the vegetables, flowers, and herbs featured in Chapter 6 are ideally suited for the summer growing season and, depending on where you live, should be started from seed in late winter or early spring. Gardeners in warm climates can directly sow their seeds in the garden, whereas gardeners in cold climates will have to start their seeds indoors.

If you are planting your garden with transplants purchased from a local grower, it generally follows that the vegetables, flowers, and herbs available for sale in your area are in season and ready to be planted in the garden at the time of purchase. When tomato plants are on sale at your local nursery or farmers' market, it is the appropriate time to plant them in your garden.

PREPPING YOUR SOIL FOR PLANTING

At the start of each new growing season, after all the annuals from the previous season have been removed and any cover crops have been cut down, I top off my raised beds with a 1-inch layer of well-finished compost. I use a hoe to lightly mix this new top layer into the existing soil to a depth of 1 or 2 inches. After the compost has been lightly tilled in, I water the bed by hand once a day for at least a week—sometimes longer, if it's too hot out to plant. While I do not drench my beds during this soil prep time, I do try to keep the soil cool and moist, so that the nutrients in the compost have a chance to begin breaking down.

I follow a similar approach for my containers—I top off each pot with a fresh layer of well-finished compost, which I then scatter with an organic all-purpose fertilizer. (Since the nutrients in the soil in a container garden are regularly washed out of the pot, it is important to add a balanced organic fertilizer to the soil.) After lightly working this new top layer into the existing soil in the pots, I water each one by hand once a day for up to a week before planting.

If you are starting a new garden, refer to Chapter 4 for information on preparing your soil.

HOW TO SOW SEEDS AND PLANT TRANSPLANTS

It is possible to start seeds in a variety of containers, but I prefer to use individual 4-inch containers to minimize the risk of damaging the seedlings during multiple transplantings. If you start your seedlings in small containers (smaller than 4-inch pots), you will need to transplant them to larger containers after they have developed their first set of true leaves, so choosing a 4-inch pot from the start is the best idea. It is also possible to start seeds directly in the garden in mild climates, or after the ground has thawed in cold regions.

I generally use individual plastic pots, which retain moisture well, though it is also possible to start seeds in peat pots and paper pots that can then be planted directly in the garden. You can recycle your plastic seedling containers for many years; however, you'll need to clean them after use each year. Wash them in a 10 percent solution of household bleach (1 part bleach to 9 parts water) to prevent the spread of disease.

I fill my seed containers with a mix of 2 parts peat moss to 1 part well-finished compost. I also add a small amount of organic all-purpose fertilizer and greensand to this mix. I blend my seed-starting mix on a large tarp, although a wheelbarrow is also a handy option. After mixing up all of the ingredients, I water it by hand—I don't drench it, but I'm certain to get it nice and evenly moist. Once watered, it's ready to go into my seed containers. I pour my seed-starting mix into each container until it overflows, and then I scrape off the excess. I never pack down the soil in the containers, because I want to allow for good airflow.

If you are unable to mix your own seed-starting mix, you can purchase a commercial seedling mix—just be sure it's something organic, untreated, and unfertilized. It should be mostly peat moss, brownish in color, and very light in weight.

Once your containers are filled with seed-starting mix, you are ready to sow your seeds. For medium and large seeds, place three seeds 1 inch apart in a single container. (You can snip off the weaker seedlings later.) Medium and large seeds should be planted three times as deep as they are wide (that's *wide,* not long). For small and tiny seeds, simply scatter them evenly across the surface of the container and then pat them lightly so that they are in good contact with the seed-starting mix.

Set the individual seed containers in shallow trays of water and let them soak until the surface of the seed-starting mix looks moist. The seed containers must remain constantly moist until the plants are up, and then they should be watered by hand at least once a day until the first set of true leaves develops. It sounds simple enough, but seedling containers can dry out surprisingly quickly. They hold only a small amount of material, so they hold an even smaller amount of moisture. If you're not on top of it, your mix will dry out and your seeds won't germinate at all.

HANDLE WITH CARE. Always hold a seedling by its root-ball or its leaves, not its delicate stem.

Seedlings also need light—a minimum of 12 and up to 16 hours of bright light each day. Place your seed containers in a spot that gets full sun. If seedlings don't get enough light, they will soon become leggy and weak and difficult to transplant. Once your seedlings have a minimum of two sets of true leaves, they can be transplanted into the garden. Be gentle with all seedlings: Handle the little plants by the soil surrounding their root clumps or leaves, rather than by their stems, and never squeeze them tightly. They will grow new leaves and roots, but they can't develop new stems.

Seedlings started indoors will need to be hardened off for at least 2 weeks before they're planted outside in the garden. Hardening off allows the seedlings to adjust gradually to outdoor conditions. Plants should be moved to a partly shady location that's 45° to 50°F. If that location is outdoors, plants should be protected from wind while hardening off.

If you're sowing seeds directly in the garden, check your seed packages to find out when to sow. Some vegetables and herbs (such as leeks, parsley, and peas) prefer cool weather, whereas others (such as basil and tomatoes) need warm soil to germinate. Plant medium and large seeds individually, three times as deep as they are wide (again, that's *wide*, not long). People often push their finger into the ground and drop in a seed. There's

MY SEEDS DIDN'T SPROUT!

Poor germination of seeds may result from seeds that are too old, poorly stored, or planted too deeply. Soil that is too cold, too hot, too wet, or too dry can also be to blame, as can insufficient light.

no way something sunk so deep is going to germinate. For most seeds, you are going down $\frac{1}{2}$ inch, at most. For carrots, lettuce, and anything that is really tiny, you are literally just scattering the seeds evenly on the surface of the soil and then patting them lightly so that they are in good contact with the soil. Don't make it any harder on your seeds than it needs to be!

Water gently after planting seeds directly in the garden, being careful not to wash anything away. Keep the soil evenly moist until the seedlings emerge from the ground, and once they're up, water at least once a day until the first set of true leaves develops. If you sowed more seeds than you have use for, thin out the weaker-looking seedlings by cutting them off at ground level with scissors when they are 2 to 3 inches tall.

When planting transplants in the garden, dig a hole in the soil about as deep as the nursery container of the plant to be planted. (Plant tomatoes deeper, so that roots develop along their stems. See page 91 for details.) Thoroughly water the transplants while they're still in their pots, then squeeze them out of their nursery pots and try to keep the soil ball intact. If there is a thick mat of roots at the bottom, loosen the roots carefully with your fingers. Place the plant and its soil ball in the prepared hole, and tamp the soil lightly with your hand. When everything is planted, water gently. If at all possible, plant on a cloudy day or in the early evening, as tender leaves burn easily.

If you're planting transplants in containers, fill the containers up to about 3 inches from the top with your potting soil mix (see page 25 for how to make a good mix), and then water the containers thoroughly. When planting in large containers, it is important to cover the drainage hole with pebbles or broken shards of pottery to make sure that it does not get blocked with soil and prevent free drainage. Then follow the same steps for planting transplants in the garden—scoop out a hole, water and remove the plant from its pot, gently cover the root-ball, and water.

Never press down on the soil around a transplant, either in the garden or in a container. If the soil is compacted, the roots can't breathe.

After planting transplants in the garden, either in raised beds or in containers, you can protect them from excessive sun or frost with a floating row cover made from either Reemay or spun polyester cloth; do this until they are well established and have doubled in size. Floating row covers will also protect seedlings and transplants from insects.

The following sample garden plans will show you a variety of great vegetable, flower, and herb combinations, as well as give you an idea of how close to space your plants in an intensively planted garden. See Chapter 6: A Gallery of Plants and Amazing Produce for detailed information on specific plants.

SUMMER GARDEN FOR TWO PEOPLE

The number in parentheses indicates the total number of plants in the raised beds. Any open spaces should be planted with nonedible flowers, such as salvias, cosmos, and zinnias.

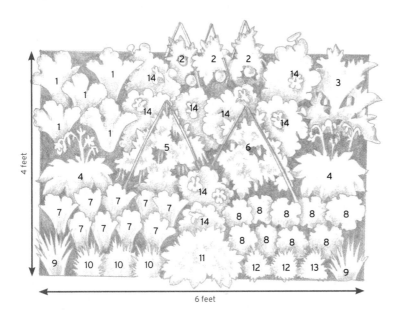

• KEY •

1. Swiss chard (5 plants)
2. Melons (3 plants)
3. Zucchini (1 plant)
4. Borage (2 plants)
5. Pole beans on teepee support (12 plants)
6. Cucumbers on teepee support (2 plants)
7. Romaine lettuce (9 plants)
8. Looseleaf lettuce (9 plants)
9. Chives (2 plants)
10. Savory (3 plants)
11. Winter squash (1 plant)
12. Tarragon (2 plants)
13. Marjoram (1 plant)
14. Nasturtiums (8 plants)

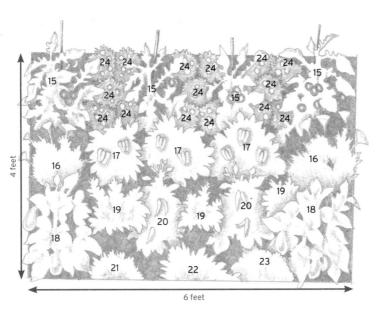

15. Heirloom tomatoes (4 plants)
16. Dill (2 plants)
17. Sweet peppers (3 plants)
18. Eggplant (2 plants)
19. Basil (3 plants)
20. Chile peppers (2 plants)
21. Oregano (1 plant)
22. Sage (1 plant)
23. Thyme (1 plant)
24. Marigolds (15 plants)

FALL AND WINTER GARDEN FOR TWO PEOPLE

The number in parentheses indicates the total number of plants in the raised beds. Any open spaces should be planted with nonedible flowers, such as cornflowers, mums, and alyssum.

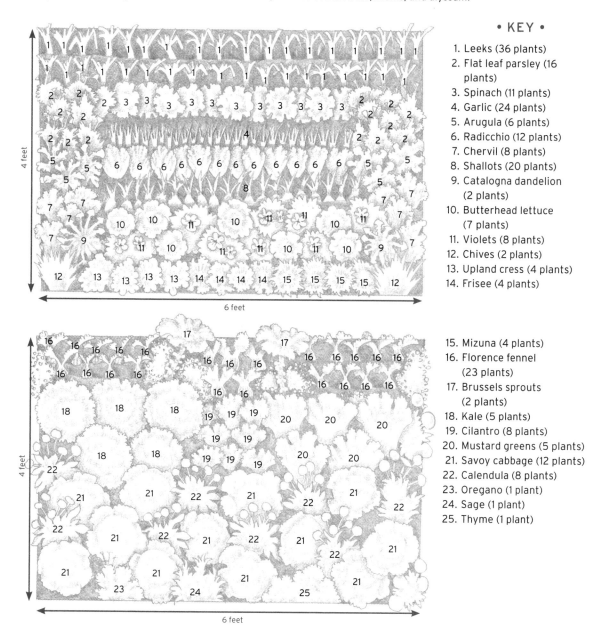

• KEY •

1. Leeks (36 plants)
2. Flat leaf parsley (16 plants)
3. Spinach (11 plants)
4. Garlic (24 plants)
5. Arugula (6 plants)
6. Radicchio (12 plants)
7. Chervil (8 plants)
8. Shallots (20 plants)
9. Catalogna dandelion (2 plants)
10. Butterhead lettuce (7 plants)
11. Violets (8 plants)
12. Chives (2 plants)
13. Upland cress (4 plants)
14. Frisee (4 plants)
15. Mizuna (4 plants)
16. Florence fennel (23 plants)
17. Brussels sprouts (2 plants)
18. Kale (5 plants)
19. Cilantro (8 plants)
20. Mustard greens (5 plants)
21. Savoy cabbage (12 plants)
22. Calendula (8 plants)
23. Oregano (1 plant)
24. Sage (1 plant)
25. Thyme (1 plant)

CONTAINER GARDEN

The number in parentheses indicates the total number of plants in the container garden design.

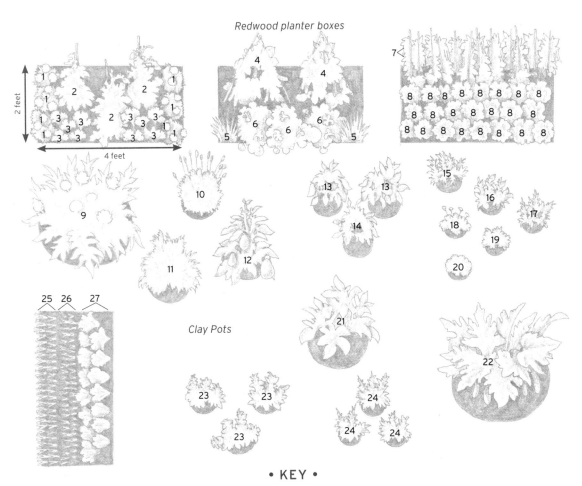

Redwood planter boxes

Clay Pots

• KEY •

 1. Marigolds (8 plants)
 2. Tomato (3 plants)
 3. Parsley (10 plants)
 4. Cucumber (2 plants)
 5. Chives (2 plants)
 6. Nasturiums (3 plants)
 7. Pole beans (12 plants)
 8. Looseleaf lettuce
    (23 plants)
 9. Artichoke (1 plant)

10. Lavender (1 plant)
11. Rosemary (1 plant)
12. Eggplant (1 plant)
13. Sweet pepper (2 plants)
14. Chile pepper (1 plant)
15. Savory (1 plant)
16. Sage (1 plant)
17. Tarragon (1 plant)
18. Marjoram (1 plant)
19. Oregano (1 plant)

20. Thyme (1 plant)
21. Potato (1 plant)
22. Zucchini (1 plant)
23. Basil (3 plants)
24. Mint (3 plants)
25. Baby leeks (48 plants)
26. Green garlic (48 plants)
27. Romaine lettuce
    (15 plants)

SHADY BORDER

The number in parentheses indicates the total number of plants in the garden bed. Any open spaces should be planted with nonedible flowers, such as foxgloves, nicotiana, and forget-me-nots.

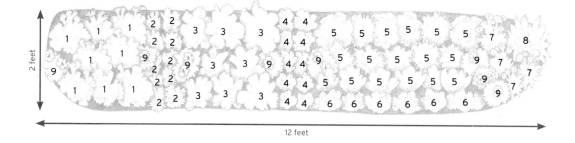

• KEY •

1. Broccoli rabe (8 plants)
2. Cilantro (10 plants)
3. Spinach (8 plants)
4. Parsley (10 plants)

5. Mixed lettuces and mizuna (17 plants)
6. Chervil (6 plants)
7. Calendula (4 plants)

8. Sorrel (1 plant)
9. Violas (8 plants)

· 6 ·

A GALLERY OF PLANTS AND AMAZING PRODUCE

Cooking is one of the most relaxing parts of my day. It's all about focusing on flavor pairings and textures. Like everyone who cooks, I have regular dishes that make up the repertoire I follow during the week. If I usually put basil in something and I don't have any, I look for a substitute flavor, perhaps marjoram or mint. That's part of cooking—always building, adapting, and changing your repertoire based on what's fresh and perfectly ripe.

The purpose of the kitchen garden is to provide a harvest of vegetables, herbs, and flowers that can be enjoyed that same day. No matter what size your kitchen garden is, it is incredibly satisfying to be involved in the entire process of creating food, from planting to cooking. The sheer variety of leaf forms and colors in your garden not only will be beautiful to look at but also will inspire you to try new things in the kitchen. You will learn to cook with ingredients as they grow and change throughout the season; you'll know, for example, what it is to eat tender young mustard greens and Russian red kale in salads and then to sauté them with garlic and red chili flakes when they have reached their prime. The quality of fresh, homegrown produce will be abundantly apparent.

Your kitchen garden should be planned around the vegetables and herbs that you enjoy most at the table, with flowers interplanted throughout. The following are some of my favorite choices for kitchen garden essentials. While most of them are warm-season plants, I've also included several perennials and cool-season plants to allow for a con-tinuous harvest.

IN THIS CHAPTER

Vegetables

Artichokes • Asparagus • Beans • Brussels Sprouts • Broccoli Rabe • Cabbage • Chard • Cucumbers • Eggplant • Florence Fennel • Garlic • Kale • Leeks • Melons • Mustard Greens • Peas • Peppers • Potatoes • Salad Greens • Shallots • Spinach • Squash • Tomatoes

Herbs

Basil • Chervil • Chives • Cilantro • Dill • Lavender • Marjoram • Mint • Oregano • Parsley • Rosemary • Sage • Savory • Sorrel • Tarragon • Thyme

Edible Flowers

Borage • Calendula • Nasturtiums • Violets

VEGETABLES

You'll note several omissions here, including root vegetables, which I generally steer my clients away from because they require lots of space for a steady, good-size yield. Why set aside so much space for beets or carrots when it's easy to buy bunches of them at the market each week? Try to fill your kitchen garden with varieties that are not easy to buy locally, that have amazing flavor when picked immediately before being eaten, and that will be attractive additions to your garden.

Artichokes

Artichokes are great ornamental edibles, with huge, silvery leaves and tasty flower buds, which, if allowed to bloom, result in large, magnificent purple blossoms. I include these beautiful plants in gardens whenever possible because they are very easy to grow. Moreover, artichokes are delicious! They have a delicate, slightly nutty flavor and a very creamy center.

Plant Family: Lettuce.

Best Climate and Site: Mild, humid coastal conditions with full sun and good ventilation; can also be grown in colder regions (Zone 6 or colder), although only as an annual. Artichoke plants are very tall and large when mature and will grow well in framed or unframed raised beds, as well as in containers that are at least 12 inches deep and that give the plants sufficient space on all sides to spread out.

Growing Season: Perennial in mild climates; summer in cold regions.

Seed to Harvest: 24 to 52 weeks for perennial varieties; 15 weeks for annual varieties.

How Much to Plant: Each full-size variety can produce up to 10 artichokes (or flower buds) per plant per season; small-size varieties can produce up to 20 flower buds per plant per season. Each plant should provide a weekly harvest for two people.

How to Grow: In mild climates, plants become better established if you transplant shoots, root divisions, or transplants in early fall so they're well rooted and reasonably large before temperatures cool during winter. Plant roots 4 inches deep, and space them 2 to 4 feet apart. Full production starts approximately 1 year after planting, although some flower buds usually develop the first spring after early fall planting. Grown as perennials, artichokes can produce well for 3 to 7 years.

In cold climates, it's best to start a short-season variety of artichoke from seed. Start seeds indoors about 2 months before the last spring frost, then move plants to a cold frame 2 weeks before the last frost to promote flower bud formation. Plant seedling roots in the garden at the level at which they grew in the pot, and space 2 to 4 feet apart.

Keep soil moist and cool, and water frequently if temperatures exceed 75°F.

Companions: Artichokes grow well with chives, garlic, sunflowers, and tarragon.

Common Problems: Aphids, earwigs, slugs, and snails.

How to Harvest: Artichokes are harvested from spring to early fall. They are at peak ripeness when their leaves are green and tight and they feel heavy for their size. For full-size varieties, use a sharp knife to cut each flower bud, leaving 2 to 3 inches of stem, when it is approximately 4 inches in diameter and still tightly closed. For small-size varieties, use a sharp knife to cut each flower bud, leaving 1 to 2 inches of stem, when approximately 2 inches in diameter and still tightly closed.

Artichokes are thought to have originated in North Africa, where they grow wild. The cultivated form has had spotty popularity, being revered by the French and ignored by the English. Nearly 80 percent of American artichoke production occurs near Castroville, California, "the artichoke capital of the world," where Marilyn Monroe was crowned "Artichoke Queen" in 1948.

Uses at the Table: While the fleshy base of each artichoke leaf is edible, the prickly tops should be discarded, along with the fuzzy choke inside. The large disk of edible artichoke found under the fuzzy choke is the creamy, delicious heart. Artichokes can be baked, braised, deep-fried, sautéed, steamed, or served raw. They pair well with butter, garlic, lemon, mint, olive oil, and parsley. A simple way to prepare full-size artichokes is to steam them whole for about 1 hour and serve them with melted butter and lemon on the side; you can also thinly slice the hearts and serve raw. Small artichokes are best braised, fried, or sautéed.

Try This Recipe: Braised Baby Artichokes, page 156.

Varieties: 'Green Globe', a full-size perennial, is the best choice for mild climates; 'Imperial Star', a full-size annual, is the best choice for cold climates; and 'Violetto di Romagna', a small-size perennial that's purple in color, is the best small-size variety for mild climates.

Tips: In cold regions, the roots of perennial artichokes can be dug up in fall and stored for replanting in spring. (If they're grown in containers, you can move the entire container to an unheated garage or shed to overwinter.) In hot regions, the entire plant can be cut down to soil level after spring production and then allowed to lie dormant (without irrigation) for several weeks. Once you resume watering it at the end of summer, new leaves and stems will quickly form in time for fall production.

Asparagus

Asparagus is a hardy perennial with tall, fernlike foliage and bright red berries. Growing your own means never having to eat tough, stringy asparagus again. Fresh asparagus has a very sweet and mild taste, and its presence is a sure sign of spring.

Plant Family: Onion.

Best Climate and Site: Asparagus can be grown in all mild to cold climates in full sun and well-drained soil, although it thrives in areas where winters are cool and the ground occasionally freezes at least a few inches deep. Asparagus takes up a great deal of space, so I recommend growing it in its own bed, either framed or unframed. Asparagus is not a good choice for containers.

Growing Season: Perennial.

Seed to Harvest: 3 years.

How Much to Plant: 12 crowns should yield enough spears for weekly harvests for two people.

How to Grow: Choose a site with full sun. The tall ferns of asparagus may shade other plants and can live up to 20 years or longer, so plan accordingly.

For best results, plant 1-year-old crowns purchased from a reputable grower or nursery. Crowns should be a grayish brown color, plump, and healthy looking. Starting asparagus from seed requires an extra year before harvest. Crowns are usually set out in late winter in milder areas or after the last frost in spring in colder areas.

Dig a trench 6 inches deep and 8 to 12 inches wide. Place the crowns 1 foot apart with their roots spread out along the bottom of the trench. Cover the crowns with 3 inches of soil. As the plants grow, continue to pile soil over the crowns until the trench is filled (approximately 2 inches of soil every 2 weeks or so). After spears shoot up in the first season, allow them to leaf out so that the foliage can nourish the growing roots and rhizomes for future production.

Each year, cut the foliage down to 2-inch stubs after the first frost or whenever the foliage yellows, and mulch lightly for winter protection.

To grow white asparagus (which has a slightly milder flavor), simply mound soil around the spears so they are protected from sunlight.

Water asparagus regularly, especially during the first 2 years. Side-dress with well-finished compost or a balanced organic fertilizer in spring and fall.

Companions: Asparagus grows well with basil, parsley, and tomatoes.

Common Problems: Asparagus beetles, fusarium wilt, and rust.

Asparagus has been a cultivated crop for millennia, popular with the Egyptians, Greeks, and Romans—both Cato the Elder and Pliny the Elder wrote about it. King Louis XVI had his gardener grow it in special hothouses, while Thomas Jefferson dedicated one entire bed at Monticello to the plant, mulching it with tobacco leaves and feeding it with manure.

How to Harvest: Harvest in spring. Asparagus spears should not be harvested the first season after crowns are planted, although they can be harvested lightly for 3 to 4 weeks in the second and third seasons, and for up to 10 weeks from the fourth season on. Once the spears are 6 to 8 inches long and the tips are closed and compact, use a sharp knife to cut them off at the soil surface.

Uses at the Table: Although the tips are the most succulent part, the whole asparagus stalk is edible. Asparagus can be blanched, grilled, roasted, steamed, or stir-fried. It pairs particularly well with balsamic vinegar, black pepper, eggs, olive oil, and Parmigiano-Reggiano.

Try This Recipe: Roasted Asparagus, page 163.

Varieties: Look for 'Jersey Knight', an all-male (and therefore more productive) green variety, and 'Purple Passion', an heirloom purple variety. (Purple asparagus turns green when cooked.)

Tips: To extend the harvest period, plant crowns at different depths: 4 to 6 inches, 6 to 8 inches, and 8 to 10 inches. The shallow plantings will come up first and can be harvested while the deeper plantings are still developing.

Beans

There are two main bean types: The first is shell beans, such as black beans, which are grown for the seeds or beans within the pod. The second is snap beans, such as green beans, which are grown for their edible pods. When growing snap beans, choose pole bean varieties over bush bean varieties because they are natural climbers and will save space in the garden. They also have a longer harvest and come in a variety of colors (including yellow and purple) and sizes, from the tiniest haricot verts to large Italian flat beans. I love to cook with different-colored snap beans, so I regularly plant heirloom pole bean varieties in my kitchen garden.

Plant Family: Legume.

Best Climate and Site: Pole beans can be grown in all regions, although they grow best in a sunny, well-drained area with air temperatures between 70° and 80°F. They can be grown in framed or unframed raised beds, as well as in containers that are at least 10 inches deep, although as natural climbers, they are best positioned along a wall or fence. If that's not possible, grow them with a teepee support.

Growing Season: Summer.

Seed to Harvest: 8 to 12 weeks.

How Much to Plant: Twelve plants should provide enough beans for weekly harvests for two people.

How to Grow: Pole beans grow by twining, so they require a support. You can make a teepee support with three or more wooden or bamboo poles that are lashed together at the top. Use poles that are at least 6 feet tall.

After the danger of frost is past in spring, directly sow four seeds 4 inches from the base of each pole, placing seeds 1 inch deep. If you're growing along a wall or fence, sow seeds in a single row, 4 inches apart and 4 inches away from the wall or fence.

Maintain even soil moisture until seeds germinate; water deeply at least once a week after plants are established.

Companions: Pole beans grow well near carrots, corn, cucumbers, lettuce, parsley, peas, and squash. Pole beans do not grow well near members of the Onion family.

Common Problems: Aphids, Japanese beetles, and Mexican bean beetles.

How to Harvest: Beans should be picked regularly to keep plants producing heavily. Use scissors to harvest beans when the pods are full-size, but before the seeds cause the pods to bulge. Leave yellow varieties on the plant until they achieve their characteristic color; purple varieties are purple from the start.

Uses at the Table: The best way to cook beans is to boil them in salted water, although they can also be sautéed, steamed, or stir-fried. Beans must be cooked long enough to develop a round, nutty, sweet flavor, so it is important to taste them as they're cooking. Beans pair well with almonds, basil, butter, and summer savory.

Try These Recipes: Braised Romano Beans with Tomato and Preserved Lemon, page 159, and Pole Bean Salad, page 142.

Varieties: For a mix of colors, I recommend 'Blue Lake', which is green and supertasty; 'Purple Pod', which is dark purple on the plant but turns light green when cooked; and 'Yellow Wax', which is yellow and has a mild flavor. I also especially enjoy 'Romano', which are wide, flat, meaty green beans.

Tips: Many bean diseases are seed-borne; try to buy seed grown in the western United States, where dry conditions make it easy for seed growers to prevent disease.

Brussels Sprouts

Resembling small cabbages, Brussels sprouts are compact buds that grow in clusters along a tall, central plant stalk. Like homegrown tomatoes, homegrown Brussels sprouts, with their sweet, nutty flavor, are far superior to anything found at the market.

Plant Family: Cabbage.

Best Climate and Site: Brussels sprouts can be grown in all regions in full sun, although they taste best when exposed to frosty weather, which allows them to develop their distinctive sweetness. They can be grown in framed or unframed raised beds and will take up a great deal of space; they are not a good choice for containers. Although slow-growing, Brussels sprouts can grow to 5 feet tall and 2 feet wide when mature.

Growing Season: Fall to spring in mild climates; midsummer to fall in cold regions.

Seed to Harvest: 14 to 15 weeks.

How Much to Plant: Two plants should provide enough sprouts for weekly harvests for two people.

How to Grow: In cold regions, set out transplants as late as possible to delay harvest until after frost. Start with the number of days to maturity of the variety you're growing, and count back that many days from your first expected fall frost date. That's the day to plant transplants in the garden. (You'll want to sow seeds 1 month before your transplanting date, either in individual 4-inch containers or directly in the garden, in warmer regions.)

In mild climates, plan for a winter-through-spring harvest. Plant transplants in the garden in late summer or early fall. Protect transplants from high temperatures for the first few weeks or until they are well established by shading them in the afternoon and watering daily, if needed.

Space 15 inches apart, either in a single row or in a 2-1-2 pattern (see illustration below). Plant companion herbs in the spaces between Brussels sprout plants.

Keep the soil moist and cool, and water frequently if temperatures exceed 75°F. Side-dress with well-finished compost or a high-nitrogen organic fertilizer, such as bloodmeal or cottonseed meal, when sprouts first form.

Companions: Brussels sprouts grow well with cilantro, dill, and fennel.

Common Problems: Aphids, cabbage loopers, club root, and flea beetles.

How to Harvest: Brussels sprouts are harvested in fall in cold regions and throughout the winter and into spring in mild climates. Sprouts develop from the bottom of the plant stalk up. For the most tender sprouts, harvest when they are roughly 1 inch in diameter and their leaves are still tightly wrapped. Remove sprouts by twisting them

2-1-2 PLANTING PATTERN. Provide sufficient space for your especially wide plants by staggering them in your bed.

from the stem. In cold regions, it's also possible to uproot the entire plant ahead of a severe freeze and then hang the stalks upside down in a cool place; you can harvest sprouts from the stalks over the next few weeks.

A cousin of kohlrabi, Brussels sprouts are so called because they first appeared (and apparently thrived) in modern-day Belgium. They are thought to be the only popular vegetable to have originated in northern Europe.

Uses at the Table: While the sprouts and leaves of the Brussels sprout stalk are both edible, the leaves are very thick and tough, and are therefore best avoided. Brussels sprouts can be boiled, braised, sautéed, steamed, roasted, or shredded raw. They pair well with butter, caraway, garlic, olive oil, thyme, and cider vinegar.

Try This Recipe: Braised Brussels Sprouts with Bacon, Garlic, and Cider Vinegar, page 157.

Varieties: 'Roodnerf' produces plump green sprouts and is quite cold-hardy. 'Rubine' is a beautiful heirloom with red leaves and red sprouts that tend to retain their color when cooked. Both are open-pollinated and produce delicious, sweet, nut-flavored sprouts.

Tips: If you have very loose, straggly sprouts, or no sprouts at all, your growing season was probably too warm. Brussels sprouts need cool weather to form their sprouts. Try planting later next season, so sprouts can form during cool fall temperatures. In mild climates, store the sprouts in the refrigerator overnight or for up to 2 days to improve their flavor.

Broccoli Rabe

Broccoli rabe, also known as rapini, is more related to turnips than it is to broccoli. It's an Italian green that produces loose, sprouting shoots with small buds that open into yellow flowers. The stems are typically peeled and eaten with the leaves and flower buds, which can be sweet to slightly bitter and peppery in taste.

Plant Family: Cabbage.

Best Climate and Site: Broccoli rabe is very fast-growing, loves cool weather, and can tolerate shade. It can be grown in framed or unframed raised beds, as well as in containers that are at least 10 inches deep.

Growing Season: Spring and fall.

Seed to Harvest: 8 weeks.

3-2-3 PLANTING PATTERN. A slightly more condensed, staggered planting pattern provides sufficient space for your midsize plants.

How Much to Plant: Twelve plants should provide enough for weekly harvests for two people.

How to Grow: Directly sow your spring crop in your garden as soon as soil temperatures are above 40°F. Once the worst of the summer heat is over, you can begin directly sowing your fall crop in your garden. In cold regions, you can continue to sow your fall crop until a month before your expected first frost. In mild climates, you can continue to sow broccoli rabe through late fall; if you mulch it, it will overwinter and produce a crop in early spring.

Sow seeds 4 to 6 inches apart, either in a single row or in a 3-2-3 pattern. (See illustration above.)

Broccoli rabe likes a steady supply of moisture, so be sure to keep the soil moist (but not soggy) throughout the growing season.

Companions: Broccoli rabe grows well with cilantro and dill.

Common Problems: Aphids, cabbage loopers, club root, and flea beetles.

How to Harvest: Harvest broccoli rabe when the flower buds are still closed and are about 1 inch across. Use shears or a sharp knife to cut stems 10 to 12 inches long. The plants

Brought to the United States by Italian immigrants in the 1920s, broccoli rabe was a weed first coaxed into cultivation by farmers in the eastern Mediterranean. It was grown not only for its edible leaves and roots, but also for the oil in the seeds, which was used for lamps.

will regularly resprout after cutting, as long as the weather remains cool. Once temperatures rise, it's best to uproot the plants and compost them, as they will quickly grow tough and bitter in warm weather.

Uses at the Table: The entire upper plant—stem, leaves, and buds, which look like miniature broccoli heads—is edible. Broccoli rabe can be sautéed, steamed, or stir-fried. It pairs well with garlic, olive oil, oregano, and red pepper flakes. One of my favorite ways to prepare broccoli rabe is to steam it for 3 minutes and then sauté it with anchovies, garlic, olive oil, and red pepper flakes. I finish it with a squeeze of fresh lemon.

Try This Recipe: Grilled Broccoli Rabe, Burrata, and Oregano Pizza, page 135.

Varieties: 'Spring Raab' and 'Sorrento' are two fast-growing varieties, both mild in flavor. 'Quarantina' is a great choice for fall harvests, with its tender, elongated leaves and pleasant, almost sweet flavor.

Tips: In hot weather, check the plants daily, as the buds quickly open into flowers. Although still edible at this point, your broccoli rabe will be much more bitter in flavor.

Cabbage

Although they take up quite a bit of space in the garden, cabbages are nevertheless beautiful additions, with their colorful and varied leaves. There are two primary types of cabbage: heading and loose-leaf varieties, including Chinese cabbages like bok choy. Of the heading types, savoy cabbage is the sweetest and most tender, and it is the one I recommend that you plant. I find its thin, ruffled leaves to be more delicate in flavor than all other cabbages, and therefore I prefer it for both cooking and eating raw in salad and slaw.

Plant Family: Cabbage.

Best Climate and Site: Savoy cabbage is the most cold-hardy of all cabbages, and it grows best in full sun. It can be grown in framed or unframed raised beds, although it will take up a good amount of space in each bed. Savoy cabbage is not well suited to containers.

Growing Season: Fall through winter.

Seed to Harvest: 14 to 16 weeks.

How Much to Plant: Each plant produces one fully formed head (and several much smaller heads after the main one is cut). Unlike other heading cabbages, savoy cabbage does not store well due to its thin leaves, so it should be eaten within 2 or 3 days of harvesting. If planted in succession, 12 plants should provide weekly harvests for two people.

How to Grow: In cold regions, directly sow seeds in the garden 12 weeks before the first fall frost. In mild regions, directly sow seeds in the garden in mid to late fall. If starting with transplants, plant out 6 weeks before the first frost in cold regions and in late fall or early winter in mild climates. Stagger plantings at 2-week intervals to extend your harvest.

Space 6 inches apart, either in a single row or in a 2-1-2 pattern for tastier, smaller heads. If planting in late summer, try to plant on the north side of a tall crop, such as pole beans or trellised cucumbers, which will provide afternoon shade.

Savoy cabbage needs a steady supply of nutrients throughout the growing season. Apply an organic liquid fertilizer such as fish emulsion with kelp or compost tea once a week for the first 3 weeks after transplanting or after seedlings break ground. Side-dress with well-finished compost, fish emulsion with kelp, or compost tea when heads start to form.

Companions: Savoy cabbage grows well with calendula, chrysanthemums, cilantro, and dill.

Common Problems: Aphids, cabbage loopers, club root, and flea beetles.

How to Harvest: A good head of savoy cabbage will be solid in the center, somewhat conical in shape, and heavy for its size; it will have deep blue-green outer leaves and a pale green center. Use a sharp knife to cut off heads at the base of the stalk.

Leave stalks and roots in place to develop a second crop of small heads.

Uses at the Table: The fully formed head of savoy cabbage is edible. It can be braised, roasted, steamed, or served raw. It pairs well with blue cheese, butter, caraway, dill, olive oil, and walnuts. Savoy cabbage is great stuffed because of its sweet flavor and its beautiful crinkly leaves. Cut and remove individual leaves off of the cabbage head and blanch them in boiling water until soft. Place cooked grains, chopped vegetables, meat, or cheese in the center of each leaf and fold over the edges to form stuffed packages. Serve immediately.

Try This Recipe: Spicy Slaw, page 145.

Varieties: 'Vertus Savoy' is very cold-hardy and produces large, light green heads. 'Famosa Savoy' is an early producer of dark green round heads. Both are perfect for cooking with, as well as for eating raw in winter slaw.

Tips: Most of the common warm-weather pests and diseases either slow down or disappear completely when the weather turns cooler, so it's okay to start your savoy cabbage from seed, even though cabbage seedlings tend to have more problems with pests and diseases than cabbage transplants do.

Chard

Chard, also known as Swiss chard, is a beautiful leafy green that continually produces over a long season without significant pest problems. Its glossy, multicolored leaves look great both in the garden and on the plate.

Plant Family: Beet.

Best Climate and Site: Swiss chard grows well in all climates and withstands cold and heat better than most greens. Plant in full sun or partial shade. It's a great choice for containers and will do just fine in framed or unframed raised beds, growing to 2 feet tall.

Growing Season: Spring to fall annual in cold regions; biennial in warm climates.

Seed to Harvest: 8 weeks.

How Much to Plant: Since you harvest individual leaves, chard will continue to produce over a long season. Six plants should produce enough leaves for weekly harvests for two people.

How to Grow: Transplant or sow directly in the garden anytime in spring after the soil has warmed to 50°F.

In mild climates, sow seeds in late summer or plant transplants in early fall for a winter crop.

Space 6 inches apart, either in a single row or in a 3-2-3 pattern. Floppy transplants will become sturdier as they grow.

Side-dress plants with well-finished compost or apply an organic liquid fertilizer such as fish emulsion with kelp or compost tea once a month throughout the growing season. Mulch around the plants with grass clippings, leaves, or straw during the hottest part of summer to keep the soil cool and moist.

Companions: Chard grows well with borage, chives, and fennel.

Common Problems: Flea beetles, slugs, and snails.

How to Harvest: Once a majority of the leaves on the plant are 6 to 8 inches long, use a sharp knife or scissors to cut individual leaves at the base of the plant, taking leaves from the outside of the plant and leaving the heart of the plant intact to continue growing. Allow the plant to double in size before harvesting from it again.

Uses at the Table: The stems and leaves are both edible, though the stems can be very thick and tough, so people often discard them. Chard can be braised, sautéed, steamed, or, if young and tender, served raw in salads. It pairs well with cilantro, eggs, garlic, lentils, olive oil, pasta, red pepper flakes, red wine vinegar, and saffron.

Try This Recipe: Braised Rainbow Chard on Toast, page 158.

Varieties: 'Bright Lights' is a rainbow variety that produces stems in an array of colors, including orange, pink, purple, red, and yellow, and it retains its color even after cooking. 'Perpetual Spinach' is an old European heirloom that is not technically spinach, though its small, tender, dark green leaves make a great spinach substitute, especially in hot climates.

Tips: Once established, chard is very cold-hardy. If regularly fertilized and harvested in mild climates, it will produce year-round for up to 2 years.

Cucumbers

Cucumbers are natural climbers, which means they can be great space savers if allowed to grow vertically on a trellis or along a fence. I typically grow one variety for eating fresh in salads and one for pickling.

Plant Family: Squash.

Best Climate and Site: Cucumbers love heat. Plant them in full sun, preferably along a fence or trellis. All varieties will grow well in framed or unframed raised beds; bush varieties grow well in containers that are at least 18 inches deep.

Growing Season: Summer.

Seed to Harvest: 8 weeks.

How Much to Plant: If well maintained and harvested regularly, each plant will produce a huge amount of cucumbers. One plant will produce enough cucumbers for two people to eat fresh daily. Another plant for pickles will be plenty for two people.

How to Grow: Transplant or sow directly in the garden as late as possible. Soil should have warmed to at least 60° and preferably 70°F.

If you're planting in a single row along a fence or trellis, space 8 inches apart. If you have the space to let your

PINCH OFF GROWTH TIPS. To save space, promote fruit production, and improve flavor, pinch off the growth tips of squash, cucumber, and melon vines anytime after they reach 4 to 5 feet in length.

cucumbers vine along the ground, plant in 1-foot-wide hills of mounded soil. Plant two vines per hill.

Try to stagger plantings, especially if you are growing pickling cucumbers in addition to slicing cucumbers. I plant my slicing cucumbers first, and then 2 to 3 weeks later I plant my pickling cucumbers, which allows me to pickle my cornichons in early fall.

Cucumbers are natural climbers, so they do not need any support once they start to climb. Growing cucumbers on a trellis or fence not only saves space, it also allows for good air circulation, which helps prevent disease problems. Trellised cucumbers are more prone to drought stress, however, as they are more exposed to the sun and air; monitor soil moisture levels regularly and water deeply.

Once the vines reach 4 to 5 feet long, you can pinch off their fuzzy growth tips to help keep the plant's overall size under control and to encourage the growth of cucumbers, rather than additional leaves.

Companions: Cucumbers grow well with nasturtiums. If grown on a trellis, cucumbers can be used to provide shade for lettuces and greens.

Common Problems: Aphids, cucumber beetles, flea beetles, and squash vine borers. Cucumbers are especially vulnerable to drought stress, which produces stunted, bitter fruit.

How to Harvest: For better-tasting slicing or salad cucumbers, harvest when they're still young, about 2 inches wide for round varieties and 6 to 8 inches long for cylindrical varieties. Gherkins should be picked when they are 1 to 2 inches long.

You can use your fingers to pinch cucumbers off the vine, although I find it much easier to use scissors.

Uses at the Table: Cucumbers can be eaten raw or pickled. They pair well with dill, garlic, mint, sour cream, all vinegars, and yogurt. For a quick pickle, I will chop a 'Straight Eight' cucumber into bite-size cubes and toss it with lots of chopped chervil, a good pinch of sea salt, and champagne vinegar just to cover. After 30 minutes in the refrigerator, it's ready to eat as a tangy sweet snack. I also love to add thin slices of cucumber to a pitcher of water and refrigerate it overnight for a delicious, refreshing drink the next day.

More than 3,000 years ago, the cucumber was already being cultivated in India. It was brought to Europe by Alexander the Great, and centuries later introduced into the Americas by Columbus.

Try These Recipes: Chilled Cucumber-Avocado Soup with Borage Blossoms, page 135, and Summer Special Salad, page 146.

Varieties: 'Lemon' is a small, round, yellow-skinned heirloom variety that is great in salads; when picked young, the skin is thin and tender. 'Straight Eight' produces slender, dark green cucumbers good for slicing. 'Cornichon de Bourbonne' is a gherkin cucumber perfect for pickling.

Tips: While I generally advocate grouping members of the same plant family together in the garden, I don't recommend this for cucumbers, which are especially vulnerable to pests and diseases. Keep cucumbers away from melons, pumpkins, and squash, and never handle wet vines. This should help minimize the spread of disease spores.

Eggplant

Eggplants are tropical shrubs that bear fruit in a range of colors, shapes, and sizes, from green to pink to red to white, from round to cigar-shaped, from $\frac{1}{2}$ inch in diameter to 1 foot long. Fresh eggplants are sweet and mild and have no trace of the bitterness often found in store-bought ones.

Plant Family: Tomato.

Best Climate and Site: Eggplants need a long, hot growing season to be productive. Plant in full sun in a spot that is protected from wind. All varieties will grow well in framed raised beds, as well as in containers that are at least 12 inches deep. Unframed raised beds can also work, especially smaller unframed raised beds, if the soil temperature remains consistently warm throughout the growing season.

Growing Season: Summer.

Seed to Harvest: 10 to 12 weeks.

How Much to Plant: Eggplant yield is closely linked to growing conditions. Should the plant suffer any water or temperature stress, yields will be greatly diminished. In cooler climates, standard eggplants should bear 4 to 6 fruits per plant; warmer climates should expect 8 to 10, and hot climates should see 12 to 15. Varieties with smaller eggplants will yield more fruit than larger-fruited varieties. Unless you're an eggplant fanatic, two plants should provide enough for weekly harvests for two people. If you're planting more than two plants, definitely try different varieties not regularly available at your local market.

How to Grow: Eggplants do not respond well to environmental stresses such as drought or cool temperatures. If you want to use transplants, be sure to get them from a reputable grower who was likely to have taken special care with them as seedlings in the greenhouse.

Starting eggplants from seed is possible, although it does require special care. Sow seeds indoors 6 to 9 weeks before the average last frost in cold regions or before

The only member of the Tomato family to have originated in the eastern hemisphere, eggplants were first cultivated in Southeast Asia 4,000 years ago. They gained wide appreciation in China and spread west, arriving in Spain after sweeping through Iran and the entire eastern Mediterranean. In the 13th century, Moors brought them to Spain, where they were alternately known as "apple of love" and "mad apple," because eating the skin was said to cause insanity. An oblong whitish variety became popular in Germany in the 1600s, leading to the English name "eggplant."

air temperatures are consistently 70°F or above in mild climates.

The soil and seeds need to stay at 80° to 90°F for the 8 to 10 days required for germination, which means you will need to provide bottom heat. Once sprouted, keep seedlings inside in a very sunny spot.

When outdoor air and soil temperatures are consistently 70°F or above, it's safe to plant eggplants in the garden.

Space 1 foot apart in a single row or in a 2-1-2 pattern. Fill the spaces between plants with companion herbs and flowers.

Once plants are established, be sure the soil is consistently moist to a depth of 3 inches; you'll need to provide 2 to 3 gallons of water per plant per week throughout the growing season to have eggplants produce fruit. Apply an organic liquid fertilizer such as fish emulsion with kelp or compost tea once a month after the first blooms appear.

Companions: Eggplants grow well with basil, cosmos, dill, and marigolds.

Common Problems: Colorado potato beetles, flea beetles, tomato hornworms, and verticillium wilt.

How to Harvest: The more you pick, the more you'll get with eggplants—meaning if you harvest consistently, you'll encourage the plants to set more fruit. Harvest when the skin is still firm and glossy. Press the skin with your finger; if it springs back, it's ready to pick. (The skin of smaller varieties may not spring back when pressed—for them, look to the color and shininess of the skin instead.) Eggplants become increasingly bitter when left on the plant—if the seeds inside have turned brown, the eggplant is past its prime. Use pruning shears to cut the stem off of the plant.

Uses at the Table: Eggplants can be broiled, fried, grilled, roasted, or sautéed. The lighter the skin color, the milder the eggplant, with white eggplants being the mildest. Eggplants pair well with cheese (especially mozzarella, Parmigiano-Reggiano, and ricotta), garlic, parsley, olive oil, tomatoes, and vinegar. Eggplant is often seasoned with rice wine vinegar in Japanese cooking and with red wine vinegar in Sicilian cooking. Salting is not necessary with fresh eggplants, though I do recommend salting eggplants for frying because it collapses air pockets in the spongy flesh, making it difficult for the eggplant to soak up excess oil when fried. To salt, cut the eggplant according to your recipe and layer the pieces in a colander, sprinkling with sea salt between layers. Let stand for 30 minutes, and then rinse well in cold water. Pat dry, and you're ready to fry.

Try This Recipe: Eggplant with Herbed Bread Crumbs and Pine Nuts, page 160.

Varieties: 'Casper White' is a compact variety that produces shiny white fruits 6 inches long with a mild flavor and firm flesh. 'Rosa Bianca' is an Italian heirloom with beautiful rose-and-white striped, teardrop-shaped fruit. 'Pingtung Long' and 'Long Purple' are thin, long, Asian varieties that are sweet and have a very creamy texture.

Tips: Eggplants don't like cold, so I never refrigerate them. Either use them freshly harvested from the garden or store them in a cool (not cold), dark place for 2 or 3 days at the most.

Florence Fennel

Florence fennel, also known as bulb fennel or finocchio, is a pale green vegetable with celerylike stems, a feathery top, and a swollen, bulblike base. Florence fennel tastes of licorice and is excellent served raw in salads in spring or braised in fall.

Plant Family: Carrot.

Best Climate and Site: Florence fennel grows well in all climates in full sun, but it does best when it matures in cool weather. It will grow well in framed or unframed raised beds, as well as in containers that are at least 10 inches deep, and it will grow to 2 feet tall.

Growing Season: Spring to fall.

Seed to Harvest: 10 to 12 weeks.

How Much to Plant: Each plant produces one fully formed bulb. If planted in succession, 16 plants should provide weekly harvests for two people.

How to Grow: Transplant or sow directly in the garden anytime in spring after the soil has warmed to 60°F. Sow seeds again in late summer for a fall crop.

Space 4 inches apart, either in a single row or in a 3-2-3 pattern.

Florence fennel can be kept on the dry side, but it shouldn't be allowed to dry out completely. Side-dress plants with well-finished compost or apply a balanced organic fertilizer such as fish

Italians distinguish between male and female finocchio and use them differently in recipes. Male plants produce compact, round bulbs, while female plants produce long, flat bulbs. The round male bulbs tend to be less stringy and therefore are the better choice for eating raw. The flat female bulbs are best when cooked.

emulsion with kelp or compost tea halfway through the growing season.

Companions: Florence fennel grows well with chard, chives, and cosmos.

Common Problems: Caterpillars.

How to Harvest: Florence fennel is harvested in late spring and again in fall. The bulbous stalk can be harvested when it is 3 inches or more in diameter. Use a sharp knife to cut the whole bulb just at the soil's surface. Fennel fronds can be cut as needed once they have reached 18 inches tall.

Uses at the Table: The bulbous stalk and feathery fronds are both edible. Florence fennel can be braised, grilled, roasted, sautéed, or served raw. It pairs well with almonds, butter, fish, lemon, olive oil, Parmigiano-Reggiano, prosciutto, and tomatoes. Thin raw slices are great tossed with olive oil, a squeeze of lemon, toasted sliced almonds, arugula, and avocado. I love to braise fennel wedges in chicken stock to serve with roast chicken in fall. Finely chopped fennel is excellent cooked in a tomato sauce.

Try These Recipes: Roasted Potatoes and Fennel with Niçoise Olives, page 164, and Shaved Fennel Salad with Arugula, Avocado, and Almonds, page 145.

Varieties: 'Zefa Fino' is a bolt-resistant variety that produces tender, compact bulbs.

Tips: For a sweeter, more tender bulb, try blanching it. When the bulbous base grows to the size of an egg, cover it with the surrounding soil. Continue to cover the bulb until harvesttime.

Garlic

Garlic is very easy to grow, and each clove planted turns into a full-size bulb. There are two types of garlic: hardneck, which tends to grow better in cold-winter areas, and softneck, which does well in areas with mild winters. Elephant garlic produces huge bulbs, but because it's not a true garlic, it is much milder in flavor. Growing your own means that you will have a steady supply of this essential kitchen staple, and it will also allow you to enjoy the sweet, tender, newly formed heads known as green garlic.

Plant Family: Onion.

Best Climate and Site: Garlic grows in all climates in full sun. It will grow well in framed or unframed raised beds, as well as in containers that are at least 10 inches deep.

Growing Season: Fall to summer.

Seed to Harvest: 40 weeks for mature heads; 8 to 10 weeks for green garlic.

How Much to Plant: Depending on how much garlic you cook with, at least 12 cloves per person.

How to Grow: Garlic must be planted in fall, anytime from October in colder regions to December in warmer regions.

Plant the largest cloves root-end down (with their papery skins still on) in the garden. In cold regions, the cloves need to be protected from frost, so they should be planted 2 to 4 inches deep. Once the soil freezes, cover it with a good 6-inch layer of leaf or straw mulch. In mild climates, plant cloves 1 to 2 inches deep.

Space individual garlic cloves 3 inches apart, either in a single row or in a 3-2-3 pattern. Space elephant garlic 6 inches apart.

Once the cloves send up green shoots in spring, fertilize them with an organic liquid fertilizer such as fish emulsion with kelp or compost tea to encourage vigorous leaf growth.

Water garlic regularly, especially in dry weather, but don't let garlic sit in soggy soil. Cut back on watering when the tops start to turn yellow.

Green garlic can be planted in spring, either directly in your garden beds or in containers. Plant individual cloves 3 inches apart and 1 inch deep. Apply an organic liquid fertilizer as soon as green shoots emerge. Water regularly, but don't let the soil get soggy.

Companions: Garlic grows well with chives, salad greens, and shallots. Members of the Cabbage family are said to stunt the growth of all members of the Onion family, including garlic. Members of the Legume family do not grow well next to chives, garlic, onions, or shallots.

Common Problems: Thrips, mildew (especially in warmer climates), and rot.

How to Harvest: Depending on when in fall it was planted, garlic is harvested from late spring through the end of summer. When the tops of your garlic plants begin to brown and fall over, carefully dig up a bulb with your hands or a spade—if the bulb is full of distinct cloves, it's ready to be harvested. Harvest all of your garlic at once. Air-cure your bulbs in a dark, dry place for 3 to 4 weeks, until the outer skins are papery. Once cured, trim the roots and neck. Softneck garlic can be braided, although I find that garlic braids tend to dry out the bulbs rather quickly. Green garlic, planted in spring, will be ready for harvest once its green shoots are at least 12 inches tall. It will resemble a leek, with a stalk about $1/2$ inch in diameter, and its skin will be soft and milky white, but a bulb will not yet have formed. Since green garlic doesn't need to be air-cured, it can be harvested on an ongoing basis, rather than all at once; just pull out the entire plant and use what you need.

Uses at the Table: The mature bulb, with its individual cloves, is edible, just as the stem of green garlic is edible. Garlic can be roasted, sautéed, or eaten raw. It pairs well with lemon, olive oil, red wine vinegar, and tomatoes. The more you cook garlic, the sweeter and mellower it gets. Green garlic is a spring delicacy—it is incredibly tender and sweet, and it can be used in place of garlic cloves. It is especially nice in a pureed soup with new potatoes and cream. Green garlic should be stored in the refrigerator, but dried bulbs should be stored at room temperature.

Some 6,000 years ago, a lucky forager in Asia dug up the bulb of a green shoot and discovered the joys of garlic. Deified by the Egyptians, used as currency in the ancient world, and applied as a talisman against evil in Central Europe, the odiferous plant is also said to have aphrodisiac powers. Dismissed as "Bronx vanilla" and "Italian perfume" by Americans who associated it with Italian immigrants in the 1920s, garlic is now recognized as an essential staple of every good cook's kitchen.

Try These Recipes: Baked Cannellini Beans with Tomato, Feta, and Dill Pesto, page 134; Braised Baby Artichokes, page 156; Braised Brussels Sprouts with Bacon, Garlic, and Cider Vinegar, page 157; Braised Rainbow Chard on Toast, page 158; Braised Romano Beans with Tomato and Preserved Lemon, page 159; Chickpeas with Tomatoes, Feta, and Herbs, page 150; Eggplant with Herbed Bread Crumbs and Pine Nuts, page 160; Grilled Broccoli Rabe, Burrata, and Oregano Pizza, page 135; Grilled Flank Steak with Chimichurri, page 151; Lamb Chops with Cilantro-Mint Yogurt Dressing, page 152; Linguine with Arugula Pecan Pesto, page 153; Little Gem Salad with Sorrel Dressing, page 141; Lemon-Oregano Vinaigrette, page 141; Mustard Greens with Cumin Seeds, page 162; Roast Chicken with Savory, page 155; Roasted Garlic, page 138; Romesco Sauce, page 139; Sautéed Cherry Tomatoes with Marjoram, page 164; and Warm Spinach Salad with Basil and Pine Nuts, page 148.

Varieties: Try a number of varieties until you find the one that grows best in your garden. In Los Angeles, where our winters are mild, I tend to grow softneck varieties. I especially like 'Chet's Italian', which has a mild flavor and can produce up to 20 cloves per bulb; 'Simonetti', with its moderate heat and large white bulbs; and 'Shantung Purple', which can be very hot and has purple-striped cloves.

Tips: I recommend buying garlic from a specialty grower rather than from the grocery store. Not only will you have a much wider selection of garlic varieties to choose from, but you will also avoid the risk of planting cloves that have been sprayed with an antisprouting chemical. For a list of specialty growers, see Resources.

Kale

Kale is a cool weather vegetable whose flavor improves significantly when the plant is exposed to frost. It is also a beautiful addition to the garden, with its variety of colors and leaf shapes. Kale and citrus are two staples I can't live without during the winter months.

Plant Family: Cabbage.

Best Climate and Site: Kale grows in all climates in full sun, though it will tolerate partial shade, especially in hot climates. Kale planted as a winter crop should be protected from wind. It can be grown in framed or unframed raised beds, as well as in containers that are at least 8 inches deep.

Growing Season: Spring to fall in cold regions; year-round in mild climates.

Seed to Harvest: 8 weeks.

How Much to Plant: When harvesting individual leaves, eight plants should yield enough for weekly harvests for two people.

How to Grow: Kale can be planted in early spring (4 weeks before the last frost) and again in late summer for a fall harvest. In mild winter regions, kale can be sown in fall for a winter harvest.

Plant transplants or sow seeds directly in the garden.

Space 6 inches apart, either in a single row or in a 2-1-2 pattern.

Kale is a heavy feeder, so you must replace soil nutrients throughout the season. Once established, side-dress plants once a month with well-finished compost or with an organic liquid fertilizer such as fish emulsion with kelp or compost tea.

Keep kale well watered to keep the leaves from getting tough and bitter.

Companions: Kale grows well with calendula, cilantro, and dill.

Common Problems: Aphids, cabbage loopers, and flea beetles.

How to Harvest: You can harvest kale at any time using the cut-and-come-again method. If I am going to be cooking with kale, I generally wait until the leaves are at

Broccoli, cabbages, and cauliflower all have a common ancestor—kale. Besides being very easy to grow, especially in cooler climates, this relatively primitive vegetable is hardy and is one of the most nutritious vegetables in the garden. The name is Scottish in origin, based on a Roman term describing cabbages.

least 6 inches long; smaller, more tender leaves are best eaten raw in salads. Use scissors to cut individual leaves from the bottom of the plant up.

Uses at the Table: Kale can be braised, sautéed, or eaten raw. It pairs well with beans, garlic, olive oil, and red pepper flakes. Stems can be very tough, so slice the leaves off before cooking. With its hearty flavor, kale is delicious in winter soups, especially with beans and sausage. Young, tender kale leaves are perfect in salads with toasted hazelnuts, blue cheese, and sherry wine vinegar.

Try This Recipe: Raw Kale Salad with Hazelnuts, Blue Cheese, and Black Mission Figs, page 143.

Varieties: 'Cavalo Nero' (also known as 'Tuscan Lacinato') has crinkled, deep blue-green leaves on stalks that can reach up to 3 feet tall. It's perfect for sautéing or in slow-cooked soups and stews. 'Russian Red' has beautiful purple-red oak-type leaves. It is both cold- and heat-tolerant. Its delicate young leaves look and taste great in salads.

Tips: Kale tastes best when picked from under a blanket of snow, and there's a scientific reason for this: A plant's carbohydrate (or sugar) reserves go into storage with the onset of cooler weather, allowing the plant tissues to withstand cold temperatures better. (In other words, sugars accumulate in the tissues and act like an antifreeze, lowering the temperature needed for the water in the tissues to freeze.) Because there's a buildup of sugars in vegetables grown in cold weather, they tend to be much sweeter-tasting than those grown in warmer temperatures.

Leeks

Leeks are the sweetest and most delicately flavored members of the Onion family. They don't take up much space in the garden, they're very cold-hardy, and they're resistant to pests and diseases, though they do require considerable time to develop. A staple of the French potager, *leeks are delicious on their own or used to infuse stock with their delicate oniony flavor.*

Plant Family: Onion.

Best Climate and Site: Leeks grow in all climates in full sun, although they will tolerate some shade. Leeks can be grown in framed or unframed raised beds, as well as in containers that are at least 12 inches deep.

Leeks will tolerate both warm and cold temperatures.

Growing Season: Spring to fall in cold regions; fall to spring in mild climates.

Seed to Harvest: 16 to 20 weeks.

How Much to Plant: If you plant 30 to 40 leeks, that should provide enough mature leeks for weekly harvests for two people. If planted in succession, 80 leeks should provide enough baby leeks for weekly harvests for two people.

How to Grow: Leeks are usually grown from transplants you start from seed. For a late summer and early fall harvest, sow leek seeds indoors in early spring and plant the 4-inch-tall seedlings in the garden 4 to 6 weeks before the last average frost date. In mildwinter climates, transplant leeks into the garden in autumn or late winter for a spring harvest. In colder climates, it's also possible to plant a second crop in early fall, although you'll need to plant a cold-tolerant variety that overwinters well.

To transplant seedlings in the garden, place each leek in a 6-inch-deep hole. (You can use the handle of a rake or hoe to poke holes in your soil.) Gently water each transplant—the water should wash enough soil into the hole to cover the roots. Subsequent watering (and rain) should fill in the holes, resulting in creamy white blanched stalks.

If you plan to harvest leeks when they're fully mature, space 3 inches apart in a single row or in a 2-1-2 pattern in containers. If you plan to harvest baby leeks, space them 2 inches apart in a single row or in a 3-2-3 pattern in containers.

Extra compost and adequate water will result in the finest leeks. Side-dress with well-finished compost twice a month throughout the growing season. Water deeply every time the soil feels dry 3 inches down.

Companions: Leeks grow well with celery, garlic, lettuce, and onions. Members of the Cabbage family are said to stunt the growth of all members of the Onion family, including leeks. Members of the Legume family do not grow well next to chives, garlic, leeks, onions, or shallots.

Common Problems: Onion maggots and thrips.

How to Harvest: You can begin harvesting leeks in late summer, as soon as they are $1\frac{1}{2}$ inches in diameter. Always use a digging fork to loosen the extensive root system before harvesting a leek plant. Leeks can also be harvested when they are much smaller; these baby leeks, which are about the size of a pencil, are perfect for braising or grilling whole.

Uses at the Table: The edible part of a leek is the white part of the stem, plus an inch or two of the pale green above it. The coarse green leaves from the stalk can be used for making stock. Leeks can be braised, grilled, roasted, or sautéed. They pair well with butter, chervil, chicken, cream, eggs, fennel, fish, Gruyère cheese, hazelnut oil, nutmeg, parsley, potatoes, and tarragon. To wash leeks, halve them lengthwise down to 1 inch from the root end, swish them around in a bowl of water to dislodge any dirt, and then soak for 10 minutes. (The dirt will sink to the bottom of the bowl.) When cooking with leeks, add them early but don't let them brown, or they'll lose their delicate flavor. I love to grill baby leeks in summer. After washing them, steam until barely tender, then brush with olive oil and season with sea salt. Grill on both sides until soft and slightly charred. Grilled baby leeks are great served with Romesco Sauce (see page 139).

Try This Recipe: Braised Leeks, page 158.

Varieties: Choose varieties that suit your climate. While long-season varieties are very cold-hardy, early maturing varieties will not overwinter in cold regions. 'Lyon' and 'Prizetaker' leeks are widely adapted English heirlooms that can grow to 3 feet tall yet remain very tender and sweet even at this large size. 'King Richard' leeks are a delicious early maturing variety. 'Blue Solaize' is a very cold-hardy leek with leaves that turn violet after a cold spell.

Tips: If you let some of your leeks go to flower, they won't be good for eating but they'll still be worth harvesting from. Use your fingers to pull off the little cloves that will sprout up around the base of each plant, and let them air-dry before planting them in the garden in spring or fall.

Melons

Although melons take up quite a bit of space in the garden, vine-ripened melons are too delicious not to grow. There are two types of melons: muskmelons, which give off a strong fragrance when ripe, and watermelons. The smaller, more aromatic French Charentais muskmelons are the best-tasting melons I've ever had.

Plant Family: Squash.

Best Climate and Site: Like cucumbers, melons love heat. Plant in full sun in the warmest part of your garden. Try to plant near a wall for the additional residual heat. Melons can be grown in framed or unframed raised beds, as well as in containers that are at least 18 inches deep. To save space, grow melons vertically on a sturdy trellis or fence; provide slings to support the fruit as it matures.

Growing Season: Summer.

Seed to Harvest: 10 to 16 weeks.

How Much to Plant: Each muskmelon vine will produce up to six fruits; each watermelon vine will produce up to three fruits. Two muskmelon and three watermelon vines should provide enough fruit for weekly harvests for two people.

How to Grow: Melons will be one of the last plants to go into your summer garden. Transplant or sow directly in the garden when the soil temperature is consistently 70°F or warmer.

If growing on the ground (that is, to spill out of the sides of your raised bed), plant melons in 1-foot-wide mounds of soil spaced 2 to 3 feet apart. Interplant nasturtiums between the mounds. You'll want up to three melon plants per mound. If growing vertically, plant melons 6 inches apart in a straight row that's 4 inches away from a sturdy trellis or fence. If growing in a container, limit yourself to two melons per 18-inch-deep pot.

In cold regions, you may want to cover your bed with black plastic in spring to warm the soil before you plant melons.

Once the vines have reached 5 or 6 feet long, pinch the growing tips off all shoots to concentrate the plants' energy on developing fruit. You can also cut off baby melons after midsummer to improve the flavor of the more mature fruit on the vines. (This is especially important to do in cold regions, where summers are short.)

If growing on a trellis, support the fruit with slings—pantyhose and onion bags both work well. If growing on the ground, prop up individual fruits to discourage rot and pest damage. (Bricks and flat rocks both make good props.)

Water plant roots with fish emulsion with kelp or compost tea every 2 weeks throughout the growing season to provide adequate nutrients and to help prevent disease problems.

Melons need plenty of water when they are young, but once the fruits have reached their full size (about 2 weeks before the listed harvest date), you should stop watering them. Too much water at ripening time ruins the flavor. Your plants will look terrible, but your fruit will be supersweet from the concentrated sugar.

Companions: Melons grow well with nasturtiums.

Common Problems: Aphids, bacterial wilts, cucumber beetles, downy and powdery mildews, and squash borers.

How to Harvest: Charentais melons must be picked when the small leaf at the end of the stem next to the fruit fades from green to pale tan. If you wait for the melon to easily

Many people believe that the best melons in the world come from where the wild versions were first domesticated—Iran and Afghanistan. A reliable source of portable water, melons spread throughout the Middle East, making their way onto the walls of Egyptian tombs and into Hebrew stories of the Exodus. When Alexandre Dumas was asked for a set of his works by the library of the French town of Cavaillon, he agreed on the provision that he be paid in melons—an annual shipment of a dozen of the town's famed Cavaillons.

pull away from the stem, it will be overripe. For watermelons, look at the bottom surface of the fruit—once the ground spot has turned a rich yellow or even orange, it's ripe for picking.

Uses at the Table: I thinly slice sun-warmed Charentais melons and serve them with prosciutto, a fruity olive oil, sea salt, and freshly ground black pepper. I love cold watermelon cut into bite-size cubes and tossed with crumbled sheep's milk feta and cracked coriander and fennel seeds.

Try These Recipes: Charentais Melon in Coconut Milk, page 166; Melon and Prosciutto, page 137; Summer Special Salad, page 146; and Watermelon with Feta, Cracked Coriander, and Fennel Seeds, page 148.

Varieties: Choose varieties that suit your climate—in cold regions, you will need to grow early maturing varieties. Charentais melons have vivid orange flesh and creamy gray skin with green stripes. 'Prior' is an early maturing Charentais melon; 'Savor' is a longer-season variety. When mature, Charentais melons weigh approximately 2 pounds. 'Golden Midget' watermelons mature very early and have yellow skin and red flesh. 'Sugar Baby' watermelons produce small, round fruit with green skin and either red or yellow flesh. All are great for growing on the ground or vertically on a trellis or fence.

Tips: Muskmelons are much more flavorful when served still warm from the sun. Watermelons are more refreshing when served chilled, although they should not be allowed to sit in the refrigerator for more than 2 days. Neither type of melon continues to ripen once picked.

Mustard Greens

Mustard greens, with their beautiful, contrasting leaves, are very easy to grow as ornamental edibles. They require very little water and develop a stronger mustardy flavor in hot weather. Mustard greens are a staple of Southern and Asian cuisines, bringing with them a spicy, peppery punch.

Plant Family: Cabbage.

Best Climate and Site: Mustard greens will grow in all climates and will tolerate both heat and light frost. Grow in full sun. Mustard greens are a great choice for 10-inch-deep containers and will do just fine in framed or unframed raised beds, growing to 2 feet tall.

Growing Season: Spring to fall in cold regions; year-round in mild climates.

Seed to Harvest: 4 to 6 weeks.

How Much to Plant: When harvesting individual leaves, eight plants should yield enough for weekly harvests for two people.

How to Grow: Transplant or sow directly in the garden in early spring and late summer. In mild climates, plant in late fall for a winter crop.

Space 6 inches apart, either in a single row or in a 2-1-2 pattern.

Side-dress plants with well-finished compost, or apply an organic liquid fertilizer such as fish emulsion with kelp or compost tea once a month throughout the growing season.

Mustard greens will grow with only limited rainfall or occasional watering. The flavor of well-watered mustard greens will not be as hot or biting.

Companions: Mustard grows well with dill, fennel, peas, and thyme.

Common Problems: Flea beetles.

How to Harvest: I wait until a majority of the leaves on the plant are 6 to 8 inches long before I begin harvesting mustard greens for cooking. Young, tender leaves can be used fresh in salads. Use a sharp knife or scissors to cut off individual leaves at the base of the plant, leaving the heart of the plant intact to continue growing. Allow the plant to double in size before harvesting from it again.

Uses at the Table: The stems and leaves are both edible, although the stems of larger leaves can be very thick and tough, so people often discard them. Mustard greens can be braised, sautéed, stewed, or eaten raw. They pair well with bacon, garlic, olive oil, sesame oil, and soy sauce. Briefly cooked, mustard greens are tender but spicy; the longer they cook, the softer their flavor becomes. I like to quickly sauté mustard greens over high heat with olive oil and lots of smashed garlic cloves. When they're just tender, I eat them on toasted bread with prosciutto.

Try This Recipe: Mustard Greens with Cumin Seeds, page 162.

Varieties: 'Red Giant' is a beautiful mustard with lime green leaves overlaid with bright purple. It tends to be a sweeter, milder variety, and it's great in salads. 'Green Wave' has dark green frilled leaves. This mustard is spicy hot, and it's perfect for braising and sautéing.

Tips: A lack of water and hot weather both sharpen the flavor of mustard greens. For greens with a more mellow flavor, try growing a fall or winter crop.

Peas

Fresh peas are truly a treat—within hours of picking, the sugars in peas start turning into starch, so the flavor and texture of fresh-picked peas is far superior to that of peas sold in the market. Pea plants come in either climbing or more compact bush varieties, and both grow better with some sort of support to wrap their tendrils around. There are three types of peas that are commonly eaten: shelling (or English) peas, snow peas, and snap peas. Shelling peas are the old-fashioned peas that are shucked from their pods and are especially tender and flavorful when eaten straight from the garden; this is the type of pea that I recommend you grow. Snow peas are flatter than shelling peas, and snap peas (a cross between the shelling and snow pea) have plump pods. The pods of both snow peas and snap peas are edible.

Plant Family: Legume.

Best Climate and Site: Peas like to grow in cool weather in full sun. Climbing varieties will need a trellis or fence to grow on; bush types will also grow on a support, though this isn't absolutely necessary. Framed raised beds and containers are better choices for peas; if you're growing in an unframed raised bed, be certain the soil is at least 40°F and dry when you plant.

Growing Season: Spring in cold regions; winter and spring in mild climates.

Seed to Harvest: 8 to 12 weeks.

How Much to Plant: It takes hundreds of shelling peas to make a side dish for even just two people. Fortunately, peas can be planted very close together, so even though you need to grow a significant number of plants in order to have any sort of meaningful yield, they don't need to take up a huge amount of space in the garden. Forty to sixty plants should provide enough shelling peas for weekly harvests for two people.

How to Grow: Snow peas, snap peas, and shelling peas all have the same growing requirements. Sow seed directly in the garden in early spring, as soon as you can work the soil in cold regions or when air temperatures are between 40° and 55°F in mild climates.

To extend your harvest, plant early maturing, midseason, and late-maturing varieties all at the same time.

Treat seeds with pea inoculant (available from seed suppliers) before planting to improve the plants' ability to fix nitrogen in the soil. This is especially important when planting peas for the first time.

Space 1½ inches apart in a single row that's 2 inches away from a fence or trellis.

Don't overwater seeds or seedlings, to keep them from rotting in wet soil. Increase watering once blooms develop.

Companions: Peas grow well with salad greens. Peas do not grow well near members of the Onion family.

Common Problems: Aphids, birds, and powdery mildew.

How to Harvest: You will want to harvest often to encourage your pea vines to continue producing. Shelling peas should be bright green and plump. The pods should feel solid but not hard when squeezed. Use your fingers or a pair of scissors to pick individual pods.

Uses at the Table: The outer pod must be removed to expose the edible peas inside. (To preserve their flavor, peas should only be shelled immediately before cooking.) Pea flowers, young leaves, and tendrils are also edible. (It is important to note that all parts of sweet peas, a completely different plant, are poisonous. Eat the flowers and leaves of only shelling peas, snow peas, and snap peas.) Shelling peas can be boiled, braised, sautéed, steamed, or eaten raw. They pair well with bacon, basil, butter, cream, and mint. Eaten straight from the garden, fresh shelling peas don't require much—they are perfectly delicious steamed for 3 minutes and drizzled with butter. For a simple lunch or afternoon snack, add a large handful of young leaves and pea tendrils to a bowl of miso soup.

Try This Recipe: Peas with Bacon, Shallots, Butter, and Dill, page 163.

Varieties: 'Alderom Pole' is a late-maturing climbing variety that reaches 5 feet tall. 'Green Arrow' is a mid- to late-maturing climbing variety that only reaches 2 to 3 feet tall. 'Laxton's Progress' is an early maturing bush variety. All produce easy-shelling pods full of plump green peas.

Tips: Your peas should be just about finished at the same time you want to start your pole beans, which means you will already have a trellis support in place for your beans to climb on. Just cut off your spent pea vines at soil level, toss them into the compost, and plant your beans.

Peppers

Both sweet and hot peppers are great additions to the summer garden. Peppers grow on compact bushes approximately 2 feet tall. There are many tasty varieties of sweet peppers beyond the usual bell peppers, including Italian sweet peppers and the small, bright red, heart-shaped 'Pequillo Pimiento'. It's also great to include one or two types of hot peppers in your garden, especially for Mexican and Asian dishes.

Plant Family: Tomato.

Best Climate and Site: Peppers are tropical plants that thrive in full sun and warm–but not hot–weather. (If temperatures are consistently above 90°F, fruit may not develop.) They will grow well in framed or unframed raised beds, as well as in containers that are at least 10 inches deep.

Growing Season: Summer.

Seed to Harvest: 8 to 12 weeks.

How Much to Plant: Three sweet peppers should provide enough for weekly harvests for two people. Hot peppers will produce a great number of fruit on each plant; if you plant one of each variety you are interested in growing, you will have plenty to cook with. Plant two of each variety if you are also interested in drying them.

How to Grow: Peppers grow best from transplants. Start pepper seeds indoors 4 to 6 weeks before you plan to plant them in the garden. Harden off seedlings for 1 week before planting–set them outside during the day, but take them back inside in the evening.

Plant transplants in the garden when soil temperatures are at least 65°F, usually about 3 weeks after the last spring frost.

Space 10 inches apart in a single row or in a 2-1-2 pattern.

Keep plants evenly moist, especially through the blossoming period, to avoid problems like blossom-end rot later. As the peppers ripen, slowly cut back on watering to improve their flavor. For extra-hot chile peppers, stop watering once the fruit has reached full size.

Peppers are shallow-rooted, so cultivate around them with care. Mulch with straw or black plastic to keep the soil temperature and moisture even.

Companions: Peppers grow well with basil, marigolds, and short varieties of sunflowers.

Common Problems: Aphids, flea beetles, tomato hornworms, blossom-end rot, and mildew.

How to Harvest: Regular harvesting encourages continued fruit production. Harvest sweet peppers when they're full size, firm, and just starting to turn color. (They will continue to ripen at room temperature.) Pick hot peppers when they are firm and glossy, before they turn soft. Use scissors rather than your fingers to cut peppers off the plant.

Uses at the Table: Peppers can be grilled, roasted, sautéed, stuffed, or eaten raw. Sweet peppers pair well with basil, garlic, olive oil, onions, sherry vinegar, and tomatoes. Peppers sautéed with garlic, onion, and olive oil are great stirred into scrambled eggs or piled on toast with fresh buffalo mozzarella. Small hot peppers, such as jalapeños and serranos, are best eaten raw. Larger hot peppers, such as poblanos, are best roasted.

Try This Recipe: Romesco Sauce, page 139.

Varieties: 'Pequillo Pimiento' is a Spanish sweet pepper that is smaller than a bell pepper. It is a beautiful deep red color and has an incredibly rich flavor when roasted. 'Nardello Sweet Italian' produces long, crinkly peppers that ripen to bright red and become perfectly creamy when sautéed. 'Purple Beauty' produces crunchy bell peppers that ripen to a deep purple and are excellent sliced raw in salads. 'Shishito' is a Japanese semihot small green pepper, delicious sautéed whole and served with a sprinkle of sea salt. 'Poblano' is a large, dark green hot chile that is perfect for stuffing and drying.

Tips: All bell peppers start out green. For colored sweet peppers, leave green peppers on the vine until they ripen and change color.

Potatoes

Freshly dug potatoes have a sweet, earthy flavor and are incredibly delicious. Potatoes are prolific growers and will produce a very decent crop in a small space. The many heirloom varieties available come in an array of shapes, sizes, and colors.

Plant Family: Tomato.

Best Climate and Site: Potatoes thrive in cool weather in full sun. They will grow well in framed or unframed raised beds, as well as in containers that are at least 18 inches deep.

Growing Season: Spring to summer in cold regions; fall to spring in mild climates.

Seed to Harvest: Potatoes come in three varieties: early season take up to 12 weeks, midseason take up to 16 weeks, and late season take up to 20 weeks to mature.

How Much to Plant: Eight plants should produce enough potatoes for weekly harvests for two people, plus extra for storing.

How to Grow: Potatoes should be started from certified disease-free "seed potatoes" purchased from a grower. (For sources of seed potatoes, see page 175.)

Cut certified seed potatoes into pieces with two or three eyes in each piece. Before planting, cure the cut pieces by spreading them out in an airy place for 24 hours. If a seed potato is the size of an egg or smaller, don't bother cutting it.

Plant your seed potato pieces directly in the garden when the soil is at least 50°F. In cold regions, plant potatoes in midspring for a summer harvest. In mild climates, plant potatoes in fall and winter for a spring harvest.

Space 10 inches apart in a single row and cover with 4 inches of soil. Interplant flowers and herbs along the length of the row, but leave open the space between potatoes for hilling.

As the vines grow, hill soil over them to keep the developing potatoes covered. Leave only the top five or six sets of leaves exposed. If you feel that you do not have sufficient soil to keep the potatoes covered, you can also use compost or straw. Once the plants blossom, stop hilling up the soil.

Potatoes grow well in framed and unframed raised beds, as well as in containers that are at least 18 inches deep. If growing in containers, put a few inches of potting soil mix in the bottom of the container, lay the seed potato pieces on the soil, and then cover the pieces with 4 inches of potting soil. (See Chapter 4 for information on potting soil.) Continue adding potting soil or compost to the container as the vines grow, always leaving the top five or six sets of leaves exposed.

Potatoes require lots of water once the leaves are fully developed and the potatoes are growing. Cut back on water when the leaves start to turn yellow to prevent the potatoes from rotting underground.

Companions: Potatoes grow well with basil, marigolds, and savory. Eggplant is an excellent trap crop for Colorado potato beetles.

Common Problems: Aphids, blight, Colorado potato beetles, flea beetles, and scab.

How to Harvest: Once the plants develop blossoms, you can begin harvesting your potatoes. This first round will be small, "new" potatoes. Gently push aside the soil around the base of each plant and pick off the potatoes with your fingers, leaving all of the very small ones on the plant. Hill the soil back over the plant to allow the remaining potatoes to develop. Once the leaves start to wither and die back, the potatoes will be fully grown. You can either harvest your fully grown potatoes all at once or, if the soil isn't too wet, you can leave them in the ground for several weeks. Wipe the dirt off of your freshly dug potatoes and allow them to air-cure in a dark, dry spot for 24 hours. Once cured, they are ready for cooking or storing.

Uses at the Table: Potatoes are incredibly versatile, although freshly dug potatoes are best enjoyed with almost nothing on them at all. Potatoes can be baked, boiled, fried, grilled, mashed, pureed, roasted, or sautéed. They pair well with butter, chives, cream, garlic, leeks, olive oil, onion, parsley, rosemary, and thyme. For an easy, incredibly delicious potato salad, cut waxy low-starch potatoes into bite-size pieces, cover with heavily salted cold water in a pot, and bring to a boil. Remove from the heat when the potatoes are still firm but tender, and drain into a colander. Toss with lots and lots of chopped fresh parsley and olive oil, cover, and let stand for 5 minutes to allow the flavors to develop. Season with salt and pepper to taste. This salad is good served warm or at room temperature.

Try These Recipes: Roasted Potatoes and Fennel with Niçoise Olives, page 164, and Sweet Corn Soup with Sage Brown Butter, page 140.

Varieties: In Los Angeles, I've had the best luck growing early maturing varieties. For cooking purposes, you'll want to consider the starch content of the potato. High-starch potatoes such as 'Burbank', 'Bintje', and 'Castle Rock' are best for baking and frying. Waxy, low-starch potatoes such as 'Red Ruby', 'Peruvian Purple', 'Yellow Finn', and all fingerling types are best for boiling and in stews, gratins, and salads. Colored potatoes will lose their color when boiled but will retain their color when cooked in stews or gratins.

Tips: Acid pine needles are a great mulch for potatoes; a more acid soil helps prevent the disease scab.

Salad Greens

Salad greens are easy to grow and so delicious when picked fresh from the garden. Growing your own from seed means you will be able to try varieties not readily available at your market. Your salad bowl will soon be filled with a new mix of textures and tastes.

Plant Family: Various.

Best Climate and Site: Salad greens like full sun in cool temperatures, but they'll also grow in warm weather if shaded. They do well in framed or unframed raised beds, as well as in containers that are at least 10 inches deep.

Growing Season: Spring to fall in cold regions; year-round in mild climates.

Seed to Harvest: Cut-and-come-again greens are typically ready to harvest in 4 weeks. Heading types, such as romaine and radicchio, are ready in 8 to 10 weeks.

How Much to Plant: A 16-square-foot area seeded with a mix of salad greens will provide enough plants for daily cut-and-come-again harvests for two people.

How to Grow: For cut-and-come-again salad greens, broadcast a mix of seeds directly in the garden as soon as the soil temperature is at least 45°F. Press seeds into the surface to make sure they have good contact with the soil, and water gently. For heading types, such as romaine or radicchio, either transplant or sow directly in the garden as soon as the soil temperature is at least 45°F. Space 5 inches apart in a single row or in a 3-2-3 pattern. To ensure an ongoing supply of salad greens, sow or transplant at 2-week intervals.

As the weather warms throughout summer, plant heat-resistant varieties in shady areas. As the weather cools in fall, plant cold-tolerant varieties, which will overwinter in mild climates. In cold regions, transplant salad greens into pots in fall so they can continue growing in a greenhouse or on a sunny windowsill.

Maintain even soil moisture, especially during the heat of summer.

Companions: Salad greens grow well with calendula, chervil, chives, garlic, and violets.

Common Problems: Aphids, slugs, and snails.

How to Harvest: Harvest salad greens in the morning to preserve their crispness. For heading types, such as romaine or radicchio, use a sharp knife to cut heads below the lowest leaves. Loose-leaf types can be harvested on an ongoing basis as soon as the leaves are at least 4 inches long. Using scissors, simply cut the outer leaves of each plant, leaving the heart of the plant intact to continue growing. Wait for the plants to double in size before harvesting from them again.

Uses at the Table: The best-tasting salads include a very wide range of greens, flowers, and herbs. Depending on what's available in my garden, my salad can include arugula, basil, borage, chives, cilantro, dandelions, dill, fennel fronds, frisée, marjoram, mizuna, nasturtium blossoms, red and green loose-leaf lettuce, sorrel, and upland cress. I toss everything with nothing more than a fruity olive oil, a squeeze of lemon, coarse sea salt, and freshly ground black pepper.

Try These Recipes: Linguine with Arugula Pecan Pesto, page 153; Little Gem Salad with Sorrel Dressing, page 141; Pole Bean Salad, page 142; Radicchio and Violet Salad, page 143; Red Quinoa Salad with Upland Cress, Arugula, Avocado, and Plums, page 144; Roasted Chicken Salad with Celery, Herbs, and Croutons, page 154; Shaved Fennel Salad with Arugula, Avocado, and Almonds, page 145; Summer Special Salad, page 146; and Warm Chicory Salad with Bacon, Pepitas, and Sherry Wine Vinaigrette, page 147.

Varieties: Arugula prefers full sun and cool temperatures and is quick to bolt in hot temperatures. The leaves are spicy and nutty in flavor, and they're best when picked young. 'Garden Rocket' produces lush leaves and, if allowed to bolt, tasty, creamy white flowers. 'Runaway' is similar to rustic or wild arugula, with small, dark green leaves and a more nutty flavor. It takes longer to germinate, but it is also much more bolt-resistant in hot weather.

Catalogna dandelion

Catalogna dandelions are not true dandelions, but rather members of the Chicory family. They prefer full sun and cool temperatures. The leaves can grow to 12 inches long, becoming dark green in color and bitter in taste. They are best picked young and tender for salads; the older, larger leaves are excellent braised.

Endive is also a member of the Chicory family. 'Frisee' is a small, frizzy endive with beautiful pale green leaves. It is only slightly bitter and is delicious with bacon and poached eggs. As with other chicories, 'Frisee' prefers full sun and cool temperatures.

Endive

Lettuces come in heading, butterhead, and loose-leaf varieties. Heading and loose-leaf lettuces tend to be more heat-tolerant than butterhead lettuces, which require cool weather. 'Rouge d'Hiver', 'Little Gem', and 'Speckled Trout' are all beautiful and tasty romaine heading lettuces. 'Merveille de Quatre Saisons' produces a gorgeous, loosely cupped butterhead lettuce with rose-pink tinged leaves. 'Rouge Grenoblaise', 'Lolla Rossa', 'Emerald Oakleaf', and 'Bronze Arrow' are all flavorful loose-leaf varieties with a mix of leaf shapes.

Mizuna is an Asian mustard green that is cold-tolerant. Its narrow, dark green leaves are sweet, with a mild mustard flavor. The leaves of red-veined mizuna have maroon streaks on them and look great in salads.

Mizuna

Radicchio is a member of the Chicory family. 'Treviso' prefers cool weather, and its burgundy-red leaves develop in color as the temperature drops. It is only mildly bitter and is good fresh in salads and even better grilled with olive oil and drizzled with balsamic vinegar.

Upland cress can be grown in cool weather. Its peppery sweet flavor is very similar to watercress.

Upland cress

Tips: Just before bolting, salad greens start to grow tall and form a bitter sap. To prevent this, pinch off the top center of the plant. Pull up and compost any greens that have gone to seed.

Shallots

Shallots are so-called multiplier onions, and they are very easy to grow. They have a sweet, delicate flavor prized in French cooking.

Plant Family: Onion.

Best Climate and Site: Shallots prefer full sun, but they'll tolerate some shade. They will grow well in framed or unframed raised beds, as well as in containers that are at least 10 inches deep.

Growing Season: Fall to spring.

Seed to Harvest: 20 to 24 weeks.

How Much to Plant: Each shallot bulb will produce a clump of up to 12 new bulbs. Fifteen to twenty bulbs will produce enough shallots for two people to cook with several times a week.

How to Grow: Plant individual shallot bulbs in the garden in fall. Push the root end of each bulb 1 to 2 inches into the soil. Mulch fall-planted shallots with several inches of leaves or straw in cold regions, and remove the mulch in early spring.

Space 4 inches apart, either in a single row or in a 2-1-2 pattern.

Once shallots have sent up green shoots in spring, fertilize them with an organic liquid fertilizer such as fish emulsion with kelp or compost tea to encourage vigorous leaf growth.

Water shallots regularly, especially during dry weather, but do not let them sit in soggy soil. Cut back on watering when the tops start to turn yellow.

Companions: Shallots grow well with salad greens. Members of the Cabbage family are said to stunt the growth of all members of the Onion family, including shallots. Members of the Legume family do not grow well next to chives, garlic, onions, or shallots.

Common Problems: Onion maggots, rot, and thrips.

How to Harvest: Once the tops have turned yellow and have started to fall over, your shallots are ready to harvest. Simply dig the entire cluster out with your hands. Carefully separate the bulbs and cure them in a dry place for 1 week before storing them for use throughout the year. Reserve the largest bulbs for planting in fall.

Uses at the Table: Shallots can be braised, fried, roasted, sautéed, or eaten raw in vinaigrettes. They pair well with butter, olive oil, thyme, and all vinegars. Shallots are essential to beurre blanc and are delicious braised whole in butter and white wine. I love to fry heaps of thinly sliced shallots in peanut oil to use as a sweet, crunchy garnish for lentil dhal.

Try These Recipes: Peas with Bacon, Shallots, Butter, and Dill, page 163; Raw Kale Salad with Hazelnuts, Blue Cheese, and Black Mission Figs, page 143; and Warm Chicory Salad with Bacon, Pepitas, and Sherry Wine Vinaigrette, page 147.

Varieties: I've had luck growing shallots that I bought at the farmers' market, but if you are interested in specialty varieties such as 'French Red' or 'French Gray', you will need to purchase sets from a supplier.

Tips: Shallot greens are delicious in salads, but be sure to leave several leaves on the plant so that the bulbs will grow normally.

Spinach

Spinach is a sweet, abundant, cool-weather green. Available with both smooth and crinkly leaves, spinach is excellent for use in salads and for cooking.

Plant Family: Beet.

Best Climate and Site: Spinach needs full sun and cool weather. It will grow well in framed or unframed raised beds, as well as in containers that are at least 10 inches deep. Be sure to move containers into shade on warm days, as soil in containers heats up more quickly than does soil in raised beds.

Growing Season: Early spring and fall.

Seed to Harvest: 4 to 6 weeks.

How Much to Plant: If cutting individual leaves, 16 plants should provide enough for weekly harvests for two people.

How to Grow: Spinach is very sensitive to warm temperatures and long days. Directly sow spinach seeds in the garden as soon as you can work the soil in early spring and again in early fall. When planting in early fall, sow seed heavily and provide lots of shade to help keep soil temperatures cool. (Germination rates decrease by half in warm weather.)

Space 4 inches apart, either in a single row or in a 3-2-3 pattern.

Once established, fertilize with an organic liquid fertilizer such as fish emulsion with kelp or compost tea every 2 weeks.

Keep soil evenly moist, and mulch with straw or compost in warm weather.

If well established in fall, spinach will overwinter even in cold regions (though it will stop growing once temperatures dip below 20°F).

Companions: Spinach grows well with chives, garlic, and tall plants such as peas and pole beans.

Common Problems: Aphids, leaf miners, slugs, and snails.

How to Harvest: Spinach can be harvested when it has at least six leaves that are 3 to 4 inches long. Cut the outer leaves with scissors, leaving at least half of the plant intact to continue growing. Allow the plant to double in size before harvesting from it again.

Uses at the Table: Spinach can be sautéed, steamed, or eaten raw. It pairs well with butter, cheese (especially feta and ricotta), cream, eggs, garlic, nutmeg, sesame seeds, all vinegars, and walnuts. Spinach sautéed in butter and seasoned with freshly grated nutmeg is outstanding on a fried egg sandwich.

Try This Recipe: Warm Spinach Salad with Basil and Pine Nuts, page 148.

Varieties: 'Bloomsdale' is a beautiful savoy-type spinach (meaning it has crinkly leaves) that is great picked young and eaten in salads. 'Giant Winter' produces large, smooth green leaves perfect for cooking.

Tips: Spinach seeds do not store well, so it's best to purchase new seeds each year.

Squash

There are two types of squash, summer and winter, although both are grown during the warm summer months. Both types take up considerable space in the garden, and both are very easy to grow. It's also possible to grow varieties not commonly found at your local market.

Plant Family: Squash.

Best Climate and Site: Squash need warm weather and full sun. Summer and winter squash both need plenty of room, though winter squash can be grown vertically to save space. Squash will grow well in framed or unframed raised beds, as well as in containers that are at least 18 inches deep.

Growing Season: Summer.

Seed to Harvest: Summer squash matures in 6 to 8 weeks; winter squash matures in 10 to 12 weeks.

How Much to Plant: Squash plants are prolific. A single zucchini plant will produce enough squash for weekly harvests for two people, plus more for baking. Winter squash can be stored for many months after harvesting, so one of any single variety will produce plenty for two people.

How to Grow: Transplant or sow directly in the garden when the soil temperature is at least 60°F. (Summer and winter squash should be planted at the same time.)

Space summer squash 18 inches apart in a single row. Winter squash can be grown along the ground or vertically. If growing along the ground (that is, allowed to spill over the sides of your raised bed), plant in 1-foot-wide mounds of soil spaced 2 to 3 feet apart. You'll want up to three plants per mound. If growing vertically, space 6 inches apart in a straight row that's 4 inches away from a sturdy trellis or fence. If growing summer or winter squash in a container, limit yourself to one plant per 18-inch-deep pot.

Once the vines of winter squash reach 5 or 6 feet long, pinch the growing tips of all shoots to concentrate the plants' energy on developing fruit. You can also cut off small squash after midsummer to improve the flavor of the more mature fruit on the vines. (This is especially important to do in cold regions, where summers are short.)

Keep soil evenly moist throughout the growing season.

Companions: Squash grows well with nasturtiums.

Common Problems: Bacterial wilts, downy and powdery mildews, squash bugs, and squash vine borers.

How to Harvest: For the best flavor and texture, summer squash should be harvested when still young—no more than 6 inches long for zucchini or crookneck, no more than 4 inches in diameter for pattypan. Winter squash must be allowed to fully ripen on the vine. When the vines have died back completely and the skin of the squash is hard, winter squash is ready to harvest. Cure all winter squash (except acorn) in the sun until the stems shrivel and turn gray. Always use either a sharp knife or pruning shears to harvest squash.

Uses at the Table: Summer squash pair well with basil, dried red pepper flakes, garlic, marjoram, olive oil, parsley, and pine nuts. I find that longer cooking brings out much more

Squash is considered by some to be a vegetable catalyst that figured in the gradual transformation of humans from hunter-gatherers to settled growers. Squash seeds found in an Ecuadorian cave have been dated to 12,000 years ago—that's 2,000 years before corn was cultivated. The name "squash" is based on the Narragansett Indian word *askutasquash,* meaning "something green eaten raw."

of their flavor. Zucchini that's slow-cooked with garlic and olive oil is delicious with fresh chopped basil, marjoram, parsley, and crumbled feta. Winter squash pair well with apples, brown sugar, butter, cloves, cumin, ginger, nutmeg, paprika, sage, and thyme. Butternut squash is perfect in risotto with Parmigiano-Reggiano and sage; delicata squash is delicious stewed with cannellini beans, rosemary, and tomatoes. Fried squash blossoms are perfect on top of pasta dishes and in salads.

Try This Recipe: Squash Blossoms with Ricotta, Mint, and Pepitas, page 165.

Varieties: I don't taste much difference in the flavors of the various summer squash, although there are considerable differences among the winter squash. For summer squash, I'm particularly fond of 'Black Beauty' zucchini, with its creamy white flesh and very dark green skin. 'Zeppelin Delicata' is a winter squash with green striped skin and a rich, sweet-potato-like flavor. Because it bears small fruit, it's a good choice for growing vertically. 'Japanese Red Kuri' produces gorgeous small, orange-red pumpkins that are great for baking.

Tips: All members of the Squash family are pollinated by insects. If you don't have a large population of pollinators in your garden, you can hand-pollinate by brushing the pollen from the male flowers (those straight from base to tip) onto the centers of the female flowers (those with a swelling at the base of the flower).

Tomatoes

Without a doubt, tomatoes are the primary reason many people plant a garden. Nothing compares to the flavor of a sun-warmed, homegrown tomato.

Plant Family: Tomato.

Best Climate and Site: Tomatoes need warm weather and full sun. Tomatoes will grow well in framed or unframed raised beds, as well as in containers that are at least 18 inches deep.

Growing Season: Summer.

Seed to Harvest: 8 to 12 weeks.

How Much to Plant: You can never have enough tomatoes! Four plants will provide enough tomatoes for daily harvests for two people, although more plants will allow you to try different varieties and will provide you with tomatoes for canning and sauces.

How to Grow: There are two kinds of tomatoes: determinate and indeterminate. Determinate tomato plants grow like a bush to a certain size (3 to 5 feet), set fruit, and then gradually decline. Indeterminate tomato plants continue to grow until frost or disease kills them; they can grow to over 8 feet tall.

Like peppers, tomatoes are most successful when grown from transplants. Start tomato seeds indoors 8 to 10 weeks before you plan to plant them in the garden. Harden off seedlings for 1 week before planting. (Set them outside during the day, but take them back inside in the evening.)

Plant transplants in the garden when the soil temperature is at least 60°F.

Dig deeper-than-normal holes for tomato transplants—you will be planting the root-ball and most of the stem. Place tomato transplants in the hole and cover the stems and lower leaves with soil so that only two or three sets of top leaves are exposed. Immediately after

PRUNE SPROUTS. Pinch off axial stems of indeterminate tomatoes.

planting, water with diluted compost tea or an organic liquid fertilizer such as fish emulsion with kelp. New roots will develop all along the buried stem, which gives the plant more stability and provides greater potential for water and nutrient absorption.

Space 18 inches apart in a single row.

Insert a stake or cage at the time of planting—use a 6- to 8-foot-tall stake or sturdy cage for indeterminate plants and a 3- to 5-foot-tall cage for determinate plants. As indeterminate vines grow, use soft twine or strips of cloth to tie them loosely to the stake at 6-inch intervals or if using a tall, sturdy cage, place the side seams on the cage supports.

Indeterminate tomatoes grown on stakes can be pruned to save space; determinate tomatoes do not need to be pruned, as they stop growing after they reach a certain size. (You can prune the lower branches off of determinate tomatoes to prevent soil-borne diseases from spreading, however.) If you look closely at how a tomato vine grows, you will see that it starts out as a single stem with leafy branches and flowering branches. Soon sprouts appear at the stem joint of each leafy branch, and they begin to grow; when sprouts are left on the plant they, too, will produce both leafy and flowering branches—first three leafy ones, then a flower cluster, then three more leafy branches, and so on. After each of these stem joints reaches three branches, pinch off its growing tip to stop further development. That way, you can keep the plant growing as a single stem. The pinching off of axial stems needs only be done every week or so.

Come mid-August, every tomato lover should give thanks to the Aztecs: They were the first people to cultivate the Nightshade superstar, around 700 AD. Moctezuma was growing them in his garden when Cortés arrived. The tomato made it to Europe with European explorers returning from the Americas in the 1500s, but it was regarded with suspicion and thought by many to be poisonous. The creation of pizza, in around 1880 in Naples, is credited with sparking an interest in the tomato. This was about the same time that the US Supreme Court ruled that it was a vegetable, not a fruit.

If you have plenty of room in your garden for tomatoes, you can trellis your indeterminate varieties. Set 6- to 8-foot-tall stakes at each end of a row of tomatoes. Starting low, when the plants are small, tie one end of a piece of twine to a stake and weave it back and forth between the plants. Tie the loose end to the other stake. Now do the same thing a little higher up, starting from the other end and making sure that you are weaving back and forth opposite the way you wove the first string; every plant should have support on both sides after you are done. As the plants get bigger, repeat this process higher up the stakes. If the row is very long, add a center support stake, otherwise your middle plants are at risk of keeling over and bringing down the whole trellis.

Side-dress tomatoes with well-finished compost or a balanced organic liquid fertilizer such as fish emulsion with kelp or compost tea as soon as the first blossoms appear.

Water management is crucial to growing tomatoes successfully. Keep the soil around new transplants moist for the first month. After that, extend the time between waterings. Water more established plants when the soil dries to 3 inches deep. Apply enough water to wet the root zone thoroughly. Frequent light watering of more established plants makes for shallow root growth and weak roots, which may result in blossom-end rot (also known as blossom-end drop). The amount of water applied later in the season has everything to do with how the tomatoes will taste. Once the fruit has reached its full size and has begun to ripen (about 2 weeks before it is fully ripe and ready to harvest), you should stop watering your plants. Too much water at ripening time ruins the flavor of the fruit. Your plants will look terrible, but your tomatoes will be supersweet from the concentrated sugar.

Companions: Tomatoes grow well with basil, marigolds, and parsley.

Common Problems: Bacterial wilts, early and late blight, nematodes, and tomato hornworms.

How to Harvest: Pick tomatoes when their color has fully developed and their skin is still firm. Use scissors to cut them from the vine. Cherry tomatoes will mature much more quickly than full-size tomatoes.

Uses at the Table: Tomatoes are incredibly versatile. They can be fried, grilled, roasted, sautéed, stewed, or eaten raw. They pair well with basil, bell peppers, black pepper, cheese, garlic, marjoram, olive oil, salt, thyme, and all vinegars. I prefer to serve large heirloom varieties fresh, with nothing more than coarse sea salt, freshly ground black pepper, basil, and olive oil. Cherry tomatoes are fantastic sautéed with olive oil, garlic, and fresh marjoram. For a quick pasta sauce, I sauté diced onions, smashed garlic, red chile flakes, and anchovies in olive oil, then add chopped San Marzano tomatoes and capers and cook for 5 minutes until the flavors have blended.

Try These Recipes: Braised Rainbow Chard on Toast, page 158; Braised Romano Beans with Tomato and Preserved Lemon, page 159; Chickpeas with Tomatoes, Feta, and Herbs, page 150; Heirloom Tomatoes with Warm Butter and Thyme, page 162; Pole Bean Salad, page 142; Radicchio and Violet Salad, page 143; Romesco Sauce, page 139; and Sautéed Cherry Tomatoes with Marjoram, page 164.

Varieties: There are literally hundreds of varieties of tomatoes to choose from. I recommend growing a variety of shapes, sizes, and colors, especially for eating fresh. 'Sungold', 'Cherokee Purple', 'Green Zebra', and 'Brandywine' (all indeterminate varieties) will make for a beautiful mixed heirloom tomato salad. San Marzano (an indeterminate variety) tomatoes are the most flavorful plum tomatoes and the best for cooking. If you do not have enough space to grow full-size tomato plants, 'Tiny Tim' is a dwarf cherry tomato that will grow in a 6-inch-deep pot.

Tips: To extend your harvest, especially in mild climates, plant a second round of tomatoes 2 to 4 weeks after your first batch.

HERBS

Herbs are an essential part of the garden, as they make good companions in the kitchen as well as in the ground. Many herbs are hardy perennials that, once established, will last for years. When buying herbs to transplant to the garden, always taste before you buy to make sure the plant has the flavor you're looking for.

To get the best flavor from your herbs, keep them from flowering. Whenever you see flower buds, pinch them off to keep the plant producing new growth instead of flowers (though you can always let one or two plants of each variety go to flower, either for your own use or to provide nectar for beneficial insects).

It's easy to air-dry herbs at the end of the summer for use throughout the winter. All you need are paper bags and string. First, cut healthy whole branches from your plants and remove any diseased leaves. Next, remove the leaves along the bottom inch or so of each branch. Use string to tie up bunches of 4 to 6 branches. Once your herb bundles are made, cut several small holes in each paper bag to allow for some airflow. Place one herb bundle upside down in each bag, then gather the open end of the bag around the bundle and tie it closed with string. Hang the bag upside down in a warm, airy room. Depending on how dry your climate is, your herbs should be dry in 2 to 4 weeks. Once dry, store in airtight containers. Dried herbs are best used within 1 year.

Also, harvest your herbs in the morning, ahead of the midday heat, to get the best flavor. Use sharp scissors or pruning shears to cut only what you have immediate need for, and your plants will continue producing throughout their growing season.

In cold regions, all herbs can be potted up in late summer or early fall and placed in a sunny window to overwinter.

While there are hundreds of different herb varieties to choose from, I find the following to be essential cooking companions.

Basil

There are many kinds of basil, including sweet and scented basils, which are used in many different cuisines around the world.

Best Climate and Site: Basil grows best in full sun, though it will tolerate some shade.

Growing Season: Summer.

How to Grow: Basil is the most frost-sensitive herb in the garden. Wait until summer has definitely arrived to transplant or sow directly in the garden.

If growing large quantities of basil for pesto, space 8 inches apart, either in a single row or in a 2-1-2 pattern. Otherwise, interplant with any members of the Tomato family.

Keep the soil evenly moist throughout the growing season.

Uses at the Table: Basil pairs well with cheese (especially mozzarella and ricotta), eggs, garlic, mint, olive oil, and oregano. Basil should be added to a cooked dish just before serving, to preserve its fresh flavor. Large-leaf varieties such as 'Genovese' and 'Purple Ruffles' tend to have sweet, milder flavors and are great in salads as well as in pesto. Cinnamon basil makes a delicious tea. Thai basil has small, anise-flavored leaves that are perfect chopped with scallions on top of cold noodles. Basil flowers are delicious in salads.

Try These Recipes: Eggplant with Herbed Bread Crumbs and Pine Nuts, page 160; Melon and Prosciutto, page 137; Pole Bean Salad, page 142; Roasted Peaches with Cinnamon Basil Sour Cream, page 170; and Warm Spinach Salad with Basil and Pine Nuts, page 148.

Chervil

Chervil is a delicate, leafy green herb with a subtle, licorice-like flavor. Along with parsley, tarragon, and thyme, chervil is a part of French cuisine's fines herbes.

Best Climate and Site: Chervil is a cool-weather crop that grows best in partial to full shade.

Growing Season: Early spring and late fall in mild climates; fall to spring in cold regions.

How to Grow: Sow chervil directly in the garden, as it doesn't transplant well.

Keep the soil evenly moist throughout the growing season.

Chervil is an excellent trap crop for slugs. I often plant it as a border for my salad greens for this reason.

Uses at the Table: Chervil pairs well with chives, eggs, fish, leeks, parsley, peas, and tarragon. Chervil is best added at the last minute, as its subtle flavor quickly disappears when cooked.

Try This Recipe: Fines Herbes Omelet, page 151.

Chives

Chives are hardy perennials that come in two varieties: onion and garlic. Onion chives have round leaves and purple flowers. Garlic chives have long, flat leaves and white flowers.

Best Climate and Site: Chives grow best in full sun. They are perfect for corners and borders.

Growing Season: Perennial.

How to Grow: Transplant or sow directly in the garden in spring in cold regions or in fall in mild climates.

Divide clumps of chives in fall every 2 or 3 years.

Uses at the Table: Chives pair well with eggs, potatoes, ricotta, sour cream, and tarragon. The flavor of garlic chives is milder than that of onion chives, with just a hint of garlic. To make chive oil, blanch a large handful of chives in boiling water for 30 seconds, and then puree in a blender with ½ cup of olive oil. Chive oil is perfect for drizzling on soups, over eggs, and on roasted potatoes. Garlic and onion chive blossoms are delicious in salads.

Try These Recipes: Chilled Cucumber-Avocado Soup with Borage Blossoms, page 135; Fingerling Potatoes with Chive Oil, page 161; Fines Herbes Omelet, page 151; and Little Gem Salad with Sorrel Dressing, page 141.

Coriander, the seed from cilantro, arrived in America with the first settlers in 1670, but it was used as far back as the Early Bronze Age. It was one of the plants grown in the Hanging Gardens of Babylon. Seeds were found in King Tut's tomb, and it is referenced in the Bible, as well as in *The Arabian Nights*. Cilantro was the original "bitter herb" used for the Hebrew Passover meal, while the Chinese believed it could make you immortal.

Cilantro

Cilantro, also known as coriander, has lemony and floral qualities and is essential to Mexican and Asian cooking.

Best Climate and Site: Cilantro grows best in full sun and cool temperatures.

Growing Season: Spring to early summer in cold regions; spring and fall in mild climates.

How to Grow: Sow directly in the garden in spring (and again in fall, in mild climates), as cilantro does not transplant well.

Cilantro is quick to bolt in warm weather. Plant in early spring and late fall in warm climates; plant in late spring and early fall in cold climates. You can also grow a more heat-tolerant variety, such as 'Delfino'.

Keep the soil evenly moist throughout the growing season.

Uses at the Table: Cilantro pairs well with avocado, chile peppers, coconut, cumin, fish, garlic, ginger, lemongrass, lime, mint, and yogurt. Add fresh cilantro at the last minute to bring a cooling note to spicy dishes such as tom kha gai or Thai coconut chicken soup.

Try These Recipes: Chickpeas with Tomatoes, Feta, and Herbs, page 150; Grilled Flank Steak with Chimichurri, page 151; Lamb Chops with Cilantro-Mint Yogurt Dressing, page 150; and Spicy Slaw, page 145.

Dill

Dill is a tall plant with fernlike leaves and delicate flower heads.

Best Climate and Site: Dill is very easy to grow and will do just fine in full sun or partial shade.

Growing Season: Spring to fall.

How to Grow: Sow directly in the garden in spring, as dill does not transplant well. Dill readily self-sows once established in the garden.

> Its flowers are great beneficial insect attractors.

> Dill grows especially well with all members of the Cabbage family.

Uses at the Table: Dill pairs well with cilantro, cucumbers, fish, mint, potatoes, and yogurt. I love to toss warm pinto beans with chopped dill, garlic, and olive oil. The immature seed heads are perfect for use in pickle recipes.

Try These Recipes: Baked Cannellini Beans with Tomato, Feta, and Dill Pesto, page 134; Little Gem Salad with Sorrel Dressing, page 141; Peas with Bacon, Shallots, Butter, and Dill, page 163; and Roasted Chicken Salad with Celery, Herbs, and Croutons, page 154.

Lavender

Lavender has beautiful gray-green leaves and produces highly fragrant purple blossoms.

Best Climate and Site: Lavender grows best in full sun in mild climates.

Growing Season: Perennial in mild climates.

How to Grow: Transplant to the garden in spring.

> Lavender can grow to 3 feet tall and is great in corners or borders.

> Lavender should be heavily pruned in fall to promote lots of new growth in spring.

> Water sparingly—lavender does not like having wet feet.

Uses at the Table: Lavender pairs well with balsamic vinegar, cream, honey, peaches, plums, and red meat. Along with basil, fennel seeds, marjoram, rosemary, summer savory, and thyme, lavender is an essential part of *herbes de Provence,* an assortment of dried herbs used as flavoring in soups and stews, and for grilled meats. Lavender blossoms and rosemary are great together in butter cookies. A little lavender steeped in balsamic vinegar is delicious over duck and quail.

Try This Recipe: Lavender and Honey Ice Cream, page 167.

Marjoram

Marjoram is much sweeter and less spicy than its cousin, oregano.

Best Climate and Site: Marjoram grows best in full sun.

Growing Season: Spring to fall; perennial in mild climates.

How to Grow: Transplant to the garden in spring, as marjoram seeds are slow to germinate.

Prune heavily in fall in mild climates to promote new leaf growth in spring.

Keep soil evenly moist throughout the growing season.

Uses at the Table: Marjoram pairs well with basil, goat cheese, parsley, summer squash, and tomatoes. I always add fresh marjoram (or marjoram blossoms) to my salad greens. It's also delicious chopped with basil and parsley, scattered on top of sliced heirloom tomatoes, and drizzled with olive oil.

Try These Recipes: Blossom Frittata, page 149, and Sautéed Cherry Tomatoes with Marjoram, page 164.

Mint

There are several mints to choose from, all with different flavors and fragrances, including apple mint, chocolate mint, lemon mint, and orange bergamot mint. Spearmint is most often used fresh, not dried, in cooking. Peppermint is commonly used in teas and candies.

Best Climate and Site: Mint will grow in partial shade to full sun.

Growing Season: Perennial in mild climates; spring to fall in cold regions.

How to Grow: Plant shoots, root divisions, or transplants in the garden in spring.

Mint is very invasive and will quickly take over a garden bed if allowed to. For this reason, I always plant my mints in their own bed and in containers.

Mint should be heavily pruned in fall in mild climates to encourage lots of new growth in spring.

Keep the soil evenly moist throughout the growing season.

Uses at the Table: Mint pairs well with basil, carrots, chocolate, cucumbers, feta cheese, lamb, peas, and yogurt. I especially like fresh mint, dill, and parsley tossed with lemon cucumbers and sheep's milk feta. Mixing chopped mint and dark chocolate into vanilla ice cream is also fantastic.

Try These Recipes: Braised Baby Artichokes, page 156; Chickpeas with Tomatoes, Feta, and Herbs, page 150; Fresh Mint Ice Cream, page 167; Lamb Chops with Cilantro-Mint Yogurt Dressing, page 152; Spicy Slaw, page 145; Squash Blossoms with Ricotta, Mint, and Pepitas, page 165; and Summer Special Salad, page 146.

Oregano

Oregano, also known as Greek oregano, is wonderfully fragrant and spicy.

Best Climate and Site: Oregano grows best in full sun.

Growing Season: Perennial.

How to Grow: Transplant or sow directly in the garden in spring.

Prune oregano heavily in fall to promote lots of new growth in spring. Like all perennials, oregano should be mulched in fall in cold regions to protect it over winter.

Once established, oregano is drought-tolerant.

Uses at the Table: Oregano pairs well with basil, bell peppers, fish, lemon, marjoram, olives, red meat, and tomatoes. For an afternoon snack, I'll put sliced heirloom tomatoes on a piece of flat bread, add crumbled feta and chopped oregano, drizzle olive oil over it, and put it in the toaster oven for 5 minutes at 350°F.

Try These Recipes: Grilled Broccoli Rabe, Burrata, and Oregano Pizza, page 135; and Lemon-Oregano Vinaigrette, page 141.

Parsley

The use of parsley originated around the Mediterranean, and it became particularly important to the Greeks. It was associated with Persephone, the goddess of spring, as well as with death, leading it to be used in wreaths and for burials. It was commonly harvested as fodder for livestock rather than for human consumption. Parsley's high chlorophyll content makes it a breath freshener, which is why it's often used as a garnish.

Parsley is either curly or flat leaf. Flat leaf is much more flavorful than curly parsley and is the best choice for cooking.

Best Climate and Site: Parsley prefers full sun and cool temperatures, but it will do just fine in partial shade in warm climates.

Growing Season: Biennial.

How to Grow: Sow directly in the garden in spring, as parsley does not transplant well.

If you use parsley on a daily basis, you will want to plant lots and lots of it to guarantee a steady supply. I tuck it in with all of my salad greens and among all members of the Tomato family.

Keep the soil evenly moist when temperatures rise.

Uses at the Table: Flat leaf parsley has a fresh, clean taste that pairs well with most savory foods, but especially with eggs, fish, garlic, and olive oil. Parsley butter is great on both grilled steaks and fish. Finely chop two large handfuls of parsley and combine with ¼ teaspoon of sea salt, a squeeze of fresh lemon juice, and a stick of room-temperature unsalted butter. Scoop the parsley butter onto a piece of parchment or waxed paper, and form it into a log. Store in the refrigerator. Slice off ¼-inch-thick rounds and place them on steaks or fish when you are grilling.

Try These Recipes: Braised Baby Artichokes, page 156; Braised Romano Beans with Tomato and Preserved Lemon, page 159; Chickpeas with Tomatoes, Feta, and Herbs, page 150; Eggplant with Herbed Bread Crumbs and Pine Nuts, page 160; Fines Herbes Omelet, page 151; Grilled Flank Steak with Chimichurri, page 151; Raw Kale Salad with Hazelnuts, Blue Cheese, and Black Mission Figs, page 143; and Roasted Chicken Salad with Celery, Herbs, and Croutons, page 154.

Rosemary

Rosemary is a fragrant evergreen shrub with a minty, piney flavor.

Best Climate and Site: Rosemary grows best in full sun.

Growing Season: Perennial in mild climates; spring to fall in cold regions.

How to Grow: Buy transplants and plant them in the garden in spring, as rosemary seeds are slow to germinate.

Summer's heat brings out more flavor in rosemary plants; the flavor is much more subtle in winter in mild climates.

Water regularly, although not too much. Rosemary does not like having wet feet.

Uses at the Table: Rosemary pairs well with beans, garlic, lamb, olive oil, and potatoes. In winter, I love to infuse honey with rosemary and drizzle it over sliced blood oranges.

Try This Recipe: Rosemary Brown Sugar Butter Cookies, page 170.

Sage

Sage, also known as culinary or garden sage, has beautiful gray-green leaves and a clean, slightly bitter taste.

Best Climate and Site: Sage grows best in full sun.

Growing Season: Perennial.

How to Grow: Buy transplants and plant them in the garden in spring. Sage started from seed takes several years to reach a harvestable size.

Sage can become quite woody after several years, so I like to replace it every 2 or 3 years.

Sage blossoms are great beneficial insect attractors.

Once established, sage is drought-tolerant.

Uses at the Table: Sage pairs well with beans, butter, chicken, thyme, and winter squash. Sage has a much better flavor when it is cooked first, either in butter or olive oil. Fried sage leaves are perfect on top of butternut squash soup or tucked into a grilled Fontina cheese sandwich.

Try These Recipes: Sage Corn Bread Pudding, page 171, and Sweet Corn Soup with Sage Brown Butter, page 140.

Savory

Savory comes in two varieties: summer and winter. Summer savory is more delicate in flavor than winter savory. Summer savory tastes like a combination of marjoram and thyme; winter savory is similar to rosemary, though not nearly as piney in flavor.

Best Climate and Site: Both summer and winter savory grow best in full sun.

Growing Season: Summer savory grows in summer; winter savory is a perennial in mild climates and grows from spring to fall in cold regions.

How to Grow: Summer savory can be sown directly in the garden in late spring. For winter savory, plant shoots, root divisions, or transplants in the garden in spring.

If grown as a perennial, winter savory will become quite woody after several years. Replace it to improve yields.

Keep the soil evenly moist throughout the growing season.

Uses at the Table: Summer savory pairs well with eggs, garlic, summer squash, and tomatoes. Winter savory pairs well with chicken, garlic, lamb, lentils, mushrooms, and potatoes. I regularly stuff a whole roasted chicken with savory, which imparts a wonderful herb flavor throughout the meat. Summer savory is great sautéed with garlic and fresh tomatoes.

Try These Recipes: Pole Bean Salad, page 142, and Roast Chicken with Savory, page 155.

Sorrel

Sorrel has bright green leaves with a very lemony flavor.

Best Climate and Site: Sorrel grows best in partial shade.

Growing Season: Perennial.

How to Grow: Sow directly in the garden in early spring.

Sorrel should be divided in fall every 2 or 3 years.

Sorrel is best in spring, when its leaves are still young and tender. French sorrel is a variety with smaller leaves and a more concentrated lemony flavor.

Uses at the Table: Sorrel pairs well with butter, crème fraîche, fish, ricotta, and spinach. When cooking with sorrel, add it at the last minute so that its color does not fade to gray. I love to heat chicken broth with sliced garlic and then add a handful of sorrel leaves to the pot. I serve this quick and delicious soup as soon as the sorrel has wilted. Chopped fresh sorrel is also excellent in salad, adding a slight tartness.

Try This Recipe: Little Gem Salad with Sorrel Dressing, page 141.

Tarragon

Tarragon, also known as French tarragon, has delicate, slender green leaves and a pronounced licorice flavor.

Best Climate and Site: Tarragon grows best in full sun, but it will tolerate some shade.

Growing Season: Perennial.

How to Grow: Tarragon cannot be grown from seed. Transplant small plants or cuttings into the garden in spring.

> Mulch around tarragon in fall in cold regions to protect it over winter.

> Keep the soil evenly moist, especially in the heat of the summer.

Uses at the Table: Tarragon pairs well with chicken, eggs, fennel, fish, mustard, and all vinegars. I love to add tarragon and shallots to my egg salad sandwiches. I will often garnish braised fennel with lightly chopped tarragon, which adds to the licorice flavor. Fresh tarragon is also great sprinkled on slices of Charentais melon.

Try These Recipes: Fines Herbes Omelet, page 151; Roasted Chicken Salad with Celery, Herbs, and Croutons, page 154; and Strawberries and Tarragon Cream, page 172.

Feeling out of sorts? Try thyme. The Sumerians were the first to discover thyme's antiseptic properties, and they used it as a disinfectant. The ancient Greeks would compliment someone by saying that they smelled of thyme. They burned thyme incense in their temples, used sprigs of thyme to preserve wine and fruit, drank thyme tea to prevent nightmares, and grew thyme to nourish their beehives. The ancient Romans gave thyme to people who seemed melancholic or shy in the belief that thyme's cheery scent could cure them.

Thyme

There are literally hundreds of varieties of thyme, although English, French, and lemon thyme are the ones most commonly used in the kitchen.

Best Climate and Site: Thyme grows best in full sun, though it will tolerate some shade.

Growing Season: Perennial.

How to Grow: Sow directly in the garden in spring or transplant divided plants in fall.

Thyme is low-growing and is therefore an excellent plant to use in borders.

Mulch thyme in fall in cold regions to protect it over winter.

English thyme has dark gray-green leaves. French thyme has narrow, pointed leaves and tends to have a stronger flavor. Lemon thyme has a distinct lemon flavor and tiny leaves ringed with yellow.

Uses at the Table: Thyme pairs well with bay leaf, chicken, corn, goat cheese, marjoram, mushrooms, onions, and savory. I always use three or four sprigs of thyme when caramelizing onions. Lemon thyme is especially nice on mixed fruit salad.

Try These Recipes: Blackberry and Lemon Thyme Sorbet, page 166; Braised Leeks, page 158; Heirloom Tomatoes with Warm Butter and Thyme, page 162; Roasted Feta with Honey and Thyme, page 137; and Roasted Garlic, page 138.

EDIBLE FLOWERS

All sorts of plants produce edible flowers, including summer squash and herbs, and I always plant a certain number of plants specifically for their flowers. Edible flowers will attract beneficial insects to your kitchen garden and will enhance the beauty and flavor of the foods you use them in.

Borage

Borage is a shaggy plant with silvery green leaves covered in softly bristled hairs and iridescent blue, star-shaped flowers.

Best Climate and Site: Borage grows best in full sun, though it will tolerate some shade, especially in warm climates.

Growing Season: Summer.

How to Grow: Sow directly in the garden in early spring.

Borage is quick to self-sow and the plants can reach 3 feet tall, so plan accordingly.

Flowers can be harvested anytime they appear.

Uses at the Table: Borage blossoms have a slight cucumber taste to them. They are perfect in salads or as a garnish on chilled soups. I freeze them in ice cubes for use in Pimm's cocktails or with sweet vermouth and a squeeze of lemon.

Try These Recipes: Chilled Cucumber-Avocado Soup with Borage Blossoms, page 135, and Summer Special Salad, page 146.

Calendula

Calendula, also known as pot marigold, has intensely bright yellow and orange flowers.

Best Climate and Site: Calendula grows best in full sun in cool temperatures.

Growing Season: Spring in cold regions; fall to spring in mild climates.

How to Grow: Sow directly in the garden in early spring or transplant in fall in mild climates.

Full-size varieties such as 'Kablouna' can grow to 2 feet tall; dwarf varieties such as 'Fiesta' average 6 to 8 inches tall. Be warned: Dwarf varieties are prone to mildew problems.

Flowers can be harvested anytime they appear. For continual blooms, remove any spent flowers.

Uses at the Table: Calendula petals have a slightly tangy flavor. Remove the petals from the flower head before using. They add color to salads and soups and are delicious (and colorful) when cooked with cumin and coriander seeds and rice.

Try This Recipe: Basmati Rice with Spices, Pistachios, and Calendula, page 156.

Nasturtiums

Nasturtiums grow in heaps of beautiful round leaves studded with orange, yellow, and red blossoms.

Best Climate and Site: Nasturtiums grow in full sun, though they will tolerate some shade, especially in warm climates.

Growing Season: Summer in cold regions; year-round in warm climates.

How to Grow: Sow directly in the garden in early spring.

The Incas used nasturtiums in their salads, but when the flower made it back to Europe with Spanish explorers, it received a less enthusiastic reception. The name comes from two Latin words meaning "nose twist," indicating the wry grimace made when first tasting the slightly spicy-bitter petals. They were particularly popular with King Louis XIV as well as Thomas Jefferson (who categorized them as a fruit, like a tomato).

Dwarf or mounding varieties include 'Alaska', with green-and-white striped leaves; 'Empress of India', with deep orange-red flowers; and 'Whirlybird', with double flowers in apricot, cream, and yellow. Climbing varieties can reach a height of 10 feet and are a good option if you have limited ground space but lots of vertical space.

Flowers can be harvested anytime they appear. Nasturtiums flower best with cool nights.

Uses at the Table: Nasturtium blossoms have a slight peppery taste to them. They are beautiful in salads and pair especially well with bitter greens such as dandelion or radicchio, shaved Parmigiano-Reggiano, and toasted walnuts. Nasturtium blossoms are also perfect for flavoring butter, especially for use with cucumber or watercress tea sandwiches.

Try This Recipe: Blossom Frittata, page 149.

Violets

All violets, including pansies and Johnny-jump-ups, come in a variety of colors and have adorable flowers with sweet faces.

Best Climate and Site: Violets grow best in partial shade.

Growing Season: Spring and fall.

How to Grow: Transplant or sow directly in the garden in early spring and again in early fall.

> Keep the soil evenly moist throughout the growing season.

> Flowers can be harvested anytime they appear. For continual blooms, remove any spent flowers.

Uses at the Table: Violets can have a slightly sweet taste. They are often sugared and used as decorations on cakes, but they're also beautiful used fresh in salads.

Try This Recipe: Radicchio and Violet Salad, page 143.

· 7 ·

MAINTAINING THE GARDEN

"Gardening is fun, but it's not a vacation." So says gardening writer Barbara Damrosch. She should know. She and her husband, Eliot Coleman, raise vegetables on a year-round organic farm in Maine.

People can be unrealistic when they estimate how much time they will have to spend in the garden. While I'm a great proponent of keeping it as simple and easy as you can, it's important to recognize that you need to be in your garden every day during the growing season, even if only for 10 or 15 minutes, to see if you have caterpillars or aphids, if your plants need to be watered, or if your food is ready to be harvested. If you're not going to use it, you'll lose it. Every yard is a microclimate unto itself, and you need to be there every day to see what's working and what isn't–particularly during the first year.

Ideally, when you're in your garden every day, you're not just watering and walking away–you're also inspecting the plants for broken stems, leaf spotting, and overnight destruction caused by insects or animals. Right now I have thrips on a garlic plant in my garden. The plant is just starting to turn yellow and is almost ready to pick; the thrips don't seem to be bothering anything else around it, so I will probably let it go. This is the sort of decision you'll make every time you go into your garden to maintain it. I encourage you to look at every plant, feel the soil, and turn over leaves, as well as water, stake and support, add shade (if necessary), and watch for pests and diseases on your daily visits. Vegetables are domesticated plants, and they do better when you pay attention to them.

Being in the garden daily also helps you notice things you may have forgotten about–edible things. While watering the other morning, I noticed two perfectly ripe 'Brandywine' tomatoes hiding behind some basil plants that had filled out after I harvested from them the week before. Without even thinking, I quickly snipped the tomatoes off the vine. They had been found, they were ready, I was hungry, and I ate.

To care for your garden, you need to perform five essential but basic tasks: watering, fertilizing, pruning and staking, harvesting, and controlling pests. (Controlling pests is discussed in Chapter 8.)

WATERING

Watering seems so easy, and yet it is the one thing we mess up the most. This comes from not touching your soil. It's just like cooking—too often people do not taste their food before putting it on a plate, though it seems logical and obvious that you should do so. Restaurant cooks, professionals who have made the same dish for years, know that you have to taste everything, every single time.

So regardless of how you water, it is important to regularly check your garden's soil moisture. Put a finger right into the soil in several locations around the garden, along the sides, as well as in the middle. If the soil is dry 3 inches down, it's time to water.

Depending on the size of your garden and the amount of time you have available to work in it, hand watering and drip irrigation are two options to consider. Hand watering is time-consuming, but it requires gardeners to work in their gardens on a regular basis, which means their gardens will be better maintained. Drip irrigation set up on timers is a very efficient means of watering and guarantees that your plants will receive the minimum amount of care necessary to grow, but it also allows you to be less attentive to your plants.

I tell my students that they should hand water for at least the first year, if possible, because they will learn so much more that way. When watering by hand, I suggest using a watering wand. They have a pleasingly precise touch that allows you to concentrate on the root zone of each individual plant as you water, even in an intensively planted bed. Wands also lessen the incidence of dirt and potentially harmful bacteria or fungi splashing onto the leaves. They are also great for watering containers and hanging baskets.

If you are watering seeds or seedlings, it is important to be as gentle as possible so you avoid washing your seeds away. I recommend using a hose nozzle that has a mist setting or, for smaller areas, a watering can with a shower-type nozzle.

Avoid directly spraying water from a hose with no nozzle, especially when you're standing over a bed and aiming down. This type of watering actually digs holes in the bed's surface (because of the pressure and steep angle), drenches the leaves, and wastes water.

EFFECTIVE WATERING BY HAND. A watering wand allows you to easily reach all nooks and crannies in the garden, which means you get water exactly where it needs to be—in the root zone.

Deep watering is important. If you only sprinkle your garden every day, water is not getting to the roots. When you are done watering, you should again dig a finger into the soil. This is the only way to know whether you're really done—if your soil is cool and moist 3 inches down, you're good to go. The ideal time to water is in the morning, before the sun is high. This avoids excessive water loss through evaporation and also gives your plants time to dry off before nightfall, which reduces the chances of diseases such as powdery mildew developing. Fungal diseases need only 2 to 4 hours of moist, warm conditions to develop.

How often you need to water will change with the weather and season. It is important to keep in mind that overwatering is a common cause of plants dying, as too much water will drown the roots. You can water less often during the cooler and wetter fall, winter, and

COLLECTING RAINWATER

Plants love rainwater! Collecting rainwater for use in your garden is as simple as connecting a rain barrel to a downspout from your roof. Collect water whenever it rains, and store it for use during the dryer months of the year. Rain barrel kits are available on the Internet, or you can contact your local Cooperative Extension for sources or instructions for building your own.

spring seasons than you do during the hot, dry summer. Don't be fooled by how your plants look. The symptoms of too much and too little water are often the same: wilting, curling, yellowing leaves. If you see these symptoms, check your garden's soil moisture first—a dry, cracked surface doesn't necessarily mean the garden is suffering. Remember, if the soil is dry 3 inches down, it's time to water.

Urban gardeners may have to deal with more pollution and residue on plants than a suburban gardener would. Dusty leaves can, in severe conditions, affect photosynthesis. To clean both sides of the leaves, you should occasionally water from overhead. You'll need to refrain from overhead watering, however, when the evenings remain warm, especially if you're watering late in the day, when leaves won't have time to dry off by sunset. Fungal diseases thrive when temperatures remain between 70° and 80°F.

Part of developing an effective watering strategy involves being honest with yourself. Can you commit to hand watering your garden? Without regular watering, nothing will grow. If hand watering, often on a daily basis, will not fit into your schedule, you should purchase a drip irrigation system or soaker hoses. They are practical alternatives to hand watering, and they deliver water directly to the plant's root zone, allowing it to seep slowly into the soil.

While there are many drip irrigation options, in many of my clients' gardens, I use $1/4$-inch plastic hoses with holes at 6-inch intervals, and I attach them to battery-operated timers. Regardless of the type of drip irrigation system you use, it should include a filter, a pressure regulator, and a backflow preventer. I also recommend including a timer so that your drip lines will go on and off at regularly scheduled times. There are easy-to-install (and affordable) drip irrigation kits available for home gardeners at nursery centers and online. (See Resources on page 175.)

WATERING CONTAINER GARDENS

In the ground and in raised beds, plants have a wide soil area from which to draw moisture. In a container, a plant has a limited soil area, and there is nothing beyond the container but air, which means that containers have a tendency to dry out fast. In the dead of summer, it is not uncommon to have to water your containers twice a day. Growing food in containers will be much easier if you can run a hose to the area where your containers are. It is also possible to water containers with a drip irrigation system; you can connect long flexible tubing to a series of offshoots for each container, and then attach the whole system to a timer to ensure that your containers get the water they need.

Even after your drip lines are set up, it is still important to regularly check your garden's soil moisture. With a properly functioning drip irrigation system, your plants should receive a long, slow watering, which allows the water to soak deep into the soil. If your soil is really wet and soggy 3 inches down, your drip lines might have sprung a leak and be flooding one particular area; drip lines can also clog, which can prevent water from reaching whole sections of your beds.

FERTILIZING

An intensively planted garden requires fertile, well-balanced soil in order to provide your plants with sufficient nutrients throughout the growing season. Plentiful additions of compost or organic all-purpose fertilizer will help keep your soil fertile.

The three basic plant nutrients needed for proper growth are nitrogen (N), phosphorus (P), and potassium (K). Nitrogen promotes healthy foliage, phosphorus promotes blooming, and potassium promotes strong roots and overall plant vigor.

Vegetables that are harvested for their fruit, such as tomatoes, will benefit from an additional feeding midway through the season. I sprinkle well-finished compost around the base of each plant and then water it into the soil just after the plants begin to blossom for the first time, to help promote good fruit set.

Vegetables grown in containers will need to be fertilized throughout the season. Once my container plants have actively started growing, I apply a liquid organic fertilizer (either fish emulsion or compost tea, depending on what I have on hand) twice a month. Because container gardens need to be watered so often, soil nutrients are regularly washed away, which means that they need to be replaced frequently.

PRUNING AND STAKING

Pruning is an often-ignored part of maintenance in the garden. Yes, plants will grow without being pruned, but too much growth can be a problem. When plants spend their energy developing leaves rather than fruit, you'll have less to harvest.

Most people know to pinch off their herbs, removing flowers to encourage bushy growth. With most flowering vegetables, you can pinch off a good one-third of the flowers to get a more flavorful, albeit reduced, yield. Sometimes, as in the case of squash, the blossoms taste as good as the fruit.

Pruning also increases airflow around plants and makes it easier to spot an insect infestation. When your garden is completely overgrown and out of control, it's hard to see what's going on with individual plants.

Pruning wanderers, such as melons and cucumbers, helps you keep control in the garden. If allowed to, most members of the Squash family will completely take over, crowding out all other plants.

I have to prune my tomatoes this weekend. I will tie up any main stalks that have started to sag under the weight of vigorous side-shoot growth, and then, if the side shoots are not flowering, I will cut them off. When pruning tomatoes early in the season, remove the lowest branches and suckers from the first few inches of the main stem. Branches with leaves low to the ground run the risk of transmitting soil diseases up the plant (and then to their neighbors).

If there is a sick plant with an identifiable disease, you want to remove it immediately so the disease doesn't spread to other plants in the same family. Take it out completely, root-ball and all, and place it in the trash, not the compost.

I like to prune as late in the day as possible, so the plant has a full night to recover. Pruning stresses a plant, so the last thing you want to do is to prune something early in the morning and then have it sitting all day in full sun, especially during summer.

Use pruning shears or sharp scissors to avoid tearing and damaging your plants. I always wash my shears with warm soapy water after pruning to avoid spreading diseases around my garden.

One of the more satisfying tasks you can perform in the garden is training plants to grow up a trellis, teepee, or other support structure. If you're strapped for room, growing vertically is the answer. By growing up rather than sideways, you can expand both the quantity and diversity of your garden plot. Send your cucumbers, melons, peas, pole beans, and squash—things that are natural climbers—up into the air wherever possible. I tie them up as soon as I get the chance, using a garlic shoot or a T-shirt cut into $1/4$-inch strips; whatever you use, make sure it's something soft and thin, but strong. Never use wire or coarse string that might cut into the plant's soft flesh; the skin on the main stalk is growing, and it's vulnerable to irritation and infection. Panty hose torn into strips, ribbons, and soft twine are all suitable, as well. If you use untreated sisal or cotton twine, you can compost it at the end of the season. Be gentle, tie loose loops, and monitor the plant's growth to make sure you're not choking or scarring it.

The most basic trellis is simply two support legs stuck in the earth, forming a V-frame over a plant and intertwined with some sort of netting, mesh, or string. These legs should be strong enough to handle heavy fruit as well as gusty winds, so sink the supports at least 10 inches into the soil. For beans and peas, you can use all types of material, from chicken wire to plastic mesh to used fishing nets. Peas and beans can easily climb 6 feet into the air, so plan accordingly. Sometimes, you must train your plants to grow a certain way—like by weaving a stem back and forth on the support, particularly at the start of the season. And be sure to place trellised vegetables on the north side of your bed so you don't shade your shorter, sun-loving plants (unless, of course, you want to create a shady spot in your garden for less heat-tolerant vegetables, such as lettuce. In this case, plant your trellised vegetables on the south side of your bed.).

SAVE SPACE BY GROWING UP. You can save space by trellising any of your natural climbers such as melon, cucumbers, winter squash, pole beans, and peas.

In my clients' gardens, I use either a flat lattice or a triangular teepee structure, both made out of bamboo. I had very limited space in one of my first gardens, so I had my client grow 'Sugar Baby' watermelons on teepees and then support the fruit with hammocks of torn-up panty hose. To do this, cut stockings into foot-long sections, knot one end, pop the fruit into the pocket when it gets to be the size of your fist, and hang the hammock on the teepee, tying each end of the hammock to a separate lattice crossbar. (If your teepees don't have crossbars, you can nail the ends of the hammocks to different vertical supports, being careful not to split the bamboo or tear the stockings.) Make sure you leave room for the watermelon to expand without encroaching on neighboring fruit. It will drop lower and lower as it grows and gets heavier, so make sure your hammock is initially high enough to account for this. And again, be sure your supports are firmly in the ground.

HARVESTING

Growing your own food allows you to eat it the same day you picked it, which means it is full of flavor and is highly nutritious. And the more you harvest, the more you'll get. Vegetables perform much better when they are submitted to ongoing harvesting. It's only by regularly picking ripe beans and peas that you'll get continual production of

CUT-AND-COME-AGAIN SALAD

Leafy greens, including arugula, chard, endive, kale, lettuces, mustard, sorrel, spinach, and upland cress can be repeatedly harvested long before their peak development.

Using scissors, snip just the amount you'll need from the outer leaves of the plant. (Leaves should be at least 4 inches long when you do this.) A good rule of thumb is never harvest more than half of the plant at one time, and then let it double in size before harvesting from it again. It helps to have three or four of each type of cut-and-come-again plant in your garden so that you can harvest from the first, and then the second, and then the third and fourth. By the time you get back to the first, it should have doubled in size and will be ready for another harvest.

flowers (and future beans and peas). If vegetables are not picked regularly, it signals the plant to stop producing.

I harvest my vegetables and herbs in the morning, before the heat of midday. I refrigerate all beans, cucumbers, Florence fennel, and greens right after picking them. I never refrigerate my eggplant, peppers, or tomatoes, and I only refrigerate my melon after cutting it. Some vegetables, such as garlic, potatoes, and winter squash, must be air-cured before you store or eat them.

"Watch your zucchini," I always warn my clients. Like all members of the Squash family, zucchini can double in size overnight and turn into something starchy, mushy, and inedible. Pick earlier rather than later. The same can be said for eggplant. If your lettuces flower and go to seed (also called bolting) in the heat, they will be too bitter to enjoy. Harvest your lettuces early and often to prevent this from happening. There are some vegetables, however, that will be just fine left on the vine or in the ground; these include garlic, kale, leeks, onions, and winter squash. I also let some of my herbs and Florence fennel flower toward the end of summer, to provide additional nectar for beneficial insects. (See individual vegetable entries in Chapter 6 for tips on when to harvest specific crops.)

One way to prevent your crops from all coming in at once is to stagger your plantings at the beginning of the season. Plant a new crop of each vegetable every 2 weeks until your beds are full. If this sounds like too much work, you can simply plant early, midseason, and late varieties of vegetables all at the same time and still enjoy a staggered harvest.

· 8 ·

CONTROLLING PESTS
AND DISEASES

When I was working at a restaurant in Los Angeles a few years ago, every so often diners would send their plate back to the kitchen because "there's a bug on it." The standard response from the owner was, "That's because we only cook organic." In reality, organic doesn't mean having to eat bugs with your lettuce. Organic means raising vegetables, herbs, and edibles in a healthy, diverse garden, without the use of synthetic pesticides or herbicides. Most of my garden clients buy organic produce already and "get" the connection between the spraying of pesticides and the foods they eat. But when their beautiful harvest is in jeopardy, they sometimes change their minds and say, "I don't care what you have to do. Just save it, and don't tell me what you did because it's better if I don't know."

In a healthy ecosystem, healthy soil produces healthy plants that can fight diseases and pests without large-scale intervention. When plants are under stress, they're unable to resist insect and disease problems. If you provide optimum growing conditions, including adequate sunlight, fertile and living soil, and sufficient water, plants will thrive.

But sometimes the growing conditions in your garden will get out of balance, and you'll find yourself having to react to any number of pest and disease problems. Even though the symptoms may show up on leaves and fruit, the first place to look is underground. Poor soil will produce weak plants that are susceptible to diseases, and that soil can be the result of too little water, too much water, too little air (soil compaction), or nutrient deficiencies. One way to ensure that your garden soil remains healthy from season to season is by adding organic material, such as compost or cover crops.

NOTICING PROBLEMS

Pests in the garden are an indication of plant stress. You'll notice signs of plant stress on leaves, stems, fruit, or roots. When you're in the garden every day, you will immediately notice when one bug suddenly becomes a dozen, or when one brown leaf leads to others that are starting to wither as well. To fully understand what ails a plant, you have to give it a slow, close inspection; look at both the infected areas and the healthy ones. Take note of what part of the plant looks sick—is it the old growth, new growth, main stem, blossoms, or fruit? Similarly, look at the plants around it, especially those in the same family. How are they doing? What's different?

WATER STRESS

When you can't tell what's causing a plant's stress by giving it a good once-over, you should always check how moist the soil is. Before you begin any watering session, always make sure the soil needs additional moisture. Overwatering is one of the most common problems my clients encounter. And unfortunately, the symptoms of too much water resemble those of too little water—a wilted, drooping plant with yellow leaves. People often mistake drowning for dying of thirst and, with the best of intentions, they make the problem even worse. Use your fingers to judge the soil's moisture content, rather than simply relying on the appearance of the plant alone. Repeat the rule: If it's dry 3 inches down, it's time to water.

NUTRIENT DEFICIENCIES

As they grow, plants draw nutrients from the soil, and this can leave garden soil depleted if nutrients are not regularly returned in the form of compost and amendments. One way to find out about nutrient levels in your soil is through direct observation of your plants.

A nitrogen deficiency is most commonly observed as a yellowing of a plant's lower leaves while the overall plant is light green. A phosphorus deficiency results in red, purple, or very dark green leaves and overall stunted plant growth. A potassium deficiency is to blame for yellow or brown leaf tips and leaf edges, weak stems, and the dropping of unripe fruit. A calcium deficiency can result in blossom-end rot and soft, black patches on fruit.

You may not be able to distinguish specific nutrient deficiencies from disease or stress symptoms, however. In general, I have found that if an entire section of my garden turns yellow at once, a nutrient deficiency is likely the cause. If one plant develops symptoms and shortly thereafter a few other plants in the same family develop similar symptoms, it is probably disease-related.

If you want to better understand what's going on with your soil, especially when you're having continuous problems, you can have your soil tested for nutrient deficiencies. Just contact your local Cooperative Extension for information on soil-testing labs.

It is important to remember that nutrient deficiencies are not common in gardens where the soil is regularly amended with compost and rock powders (see Chapter 4). If you do suspect a mineral deficiency during the growing season, a simple solution is to spray your plants with either fish emulsion with kelp or compost tea, both of which supply your plants with a broad range of nutrients. Also, maintain a consistent level of soil moisture because plants can't properly absorb nutrients from dry or soaking-wet soil.

COMMON INSECT PESTS AND PLANT DISEASES

When your plants are under stress, they are much more susceptible to insect and disease problems. If you see big holes in your leaves, that's a pretty good indication that you have an insect problem. It could be caterpillars, cucumber beetles, slugs, snails—the list is long and depressing. While plant breeders have come up with many disease-resistant varieties, there are no insect-resistant varieties available.

Aphids come in numerous varieties and sizes, but they are usually green, white, or black. With an infestation, you'll see clusters of colored dots on plant stems and leaves. These insects suck sap from plants, causing damage and transmitting viruses. Beneficial insects, especially ladybugs, will help control them. It's also possible to knock aphids off plants with spray from a hose; a strong shot of water will kill these soft-bodied pests. For really bad infestations, remove the plant altogether, especially if it is young; you should still have enough time in the season to pop in another transplant. For mature plants

loaded with vegetables, you may choose to spray with an insecticidal soap to try to sal-
vage your harvest, then wash all produce carefully before eating.

Beetles nibble on the leaves of beans, potatoes, radishes, and all members of the
Squash family, often skeletonizing leaves as they go. Cover seedlings with a floating row
cover made from either Reemay or spun polyester cloth to prevent beetles from settling
in on your crops. If you don't use a floating row cover and later find beetles feasting in
your garden, hand picking can be an effective control; just drop the beetles into a jar of
soapy water and discard them. If there are too many beetles to pick and crop damage is
severe, you can spray with a plant-derived, organic pyrethrin as a last resort.

Caterpillars are troublesome for members of the Cabbage family, especially early in
the season. Ragged edges on your leaves are a sure sign of caterpillar damage. I have
found hand picking, especially after watering or in the early evening, to be the best remedy for caterpillar populations. Though they tend to blend in perfectly with the plants
they are eating, they can usually be found on the undersides of leaves. If crop damage is
severe, you can spray your plants with Bt (*Bacillus thuringiensis*), a bacterial pest control
for caterpillars.

NOTICE THE DIFFERENCE. Beetle damage versus caterpillar damage versus slug and snail damage.

Slugs and snails love moist conditions and will eat perfectly round holes in the leaves of a wide range of plants. They also chew holes in tomatoes at or near ground level. Snails are definitely much easier to spot than slugs, but both are easily hand picked, especially at night when they are feeding. If slugs and snails are plentiful, you can spread baits containing iron phosphate on the surface of the soil.

Fungi are responsible for some common vegetable plant diseases, including blight, club root, and downy and powdery mildew. Blight affects members of the Tomato family. The leaves and branches of infected plants suddenly wither and stop growing. The fruit may also rot.

Club root commonly infects members of the Cabbage family and causes large swellings on their roots, which can stunt or even kill the plants.

The primary symptom of downy mildew is a white, downy growth on the undersides of leaves; powdery mildew appears as a powdery growth on both upper and lower leaf surfaces. Downy mildew can quickly kill your plant, whereas powdery mildew commonly causes poor plant growth, but rarely kills the plant.

One of the best ways to prevent fungal problems is to select disease-resistant varieties whenever possible. Proper garden maintenance also helps prevent fungal infections. Avoid watering your plants' leaves, especially during warm weather, and stay on top of pruning to allow for good airflow through your plantings. Crop rotation can also starve out soilborne diseases. (See page 123 for more on crop rotation.)

If your plants suffer from a fungal disease, cut off the infected part of the plant to help reduce the spread of the disease. If a plant is seriously infected (if more than half of its stems and leaves are infected), remove the entire plant, including its roots, and dispose of it in the trash.

For a complete list of insect pests and diseases in your area, contact your local Cooperative Extension.

KEEP IT CLEAN

Good sanitation plays an important role in maintaining a healthy, thriving garden, so keep your tools clean. After pruning, wash your shears with warm soapy water. Remove infected plants promptly, and do not put them in your compost bin. If you bring new plants into your garden, check them for insects and diseases before planting. You can easily see aphids and spider mites (characterized by fine white webbing and pinhead-size brownish insects) on a small plant. Turn over the leaves and inspect them carefully.

Always prune when plants are dry. Bacteria and fungi can be transferred from an infected plant to your shears or hands and then onto a healthy plant; water in any form, from droplets to dew, makes transmission easier.

COMPANION PLANTING

Companion planting for insect control means interplanting your vegetable crop with plants that will attract beneficial insects, function as trap crops, or potentially even repel pests. While companion planting is not an exact science, we do know that some plants can make good or bad neighbors for one another due to their exhalations, scents, and root excretions.

For me, using companion plants as a form of insect control works much better when I'm trying to attract beneficial insects to my garden than when I'm trying to repel the bugs I don't want to see. I regularly plant edible and nonedible flowers in my kitchen garden, with an eye toward a great mix of shapes, sizes, and colors, in order to attract a wide range of beneficial insects. You need a good mix of flowers that will attract bees to help with pollination, especially if you're planting anything in the Squash family, since they don't self-pollinate. Borage, calendula, and nasturtiums are all effective (and edible) additions. I also like putting in nonculinary salvias to attract hummingbirds, and I let a certain number of herbs go to flower each summer to provide an additional source of nectar for beneficial insects.

Certain plants function as trap crops by attracting pests and keeping them distracted and away from other plants. By offering an attractive decoy in the vicinity of an at-risk crop, such as eggplant (the trap crop) near potatoes (the at-risk crop vulnerable to the widespread Colorado potato beetle), you can reduce the chances of problem insects feasting on your preferred crop. It's important to realize that trap crops are disposable

CHIVES IN EVERY BED. Chives are perfect for filling in corner spaces and are noted for their ability to repel a number of problem insects.

and should be uprooted after they're fully infested and have served their purpose as either food or lodging for damaging insects.

Certain plants contain biochemicals that repel specific pests. Some plants exude chemicals from their roots or aerial parts that suppress or repel pests and protect neighboring plants. French and African marigolds, for example, release thiophene—a nematode repellent—through their roots, making them good companions for a number of garden crops. Chives, which are members of the Onion family, are also said to repel a variety of insects, so I plant them in everyone's garden. They have a shape that is great for corners, and they easily fill in an odd space. Best of all, they have beautiful, edible blossoms in spring.

Remember: Companion plants aren't a panacea against pests—although they can help you fight the battle. See Chapter 5 for a list of plant families and their common herb and flower companions.

BENEFICIAL INSECTS

When it comes to the battle against pests, you'll get the most bang for your buck if you work to attract good insects into your yard. In addition to the pollinators you want for reliable germination, there are also the killers: the predators and the parasites. Predators actively target your pests, while parasites let their larvae do the job. Some people even plant an insectary, a separate garden buffet dedicated to feeding and housing the good bugs, but I prefer to mix it all up in my raised beds.

There are numerous beneficial insects that should be encouraged to live in your garden, including bees, various flies, ground beetles, lacewings, ladybugs, parasitic wasps, praying mantises, and spiders. If you are putting in a garden for the first time, or if you simply want to jump-start your beneficial insect population, you can buy any number of predators or parasites at your local nursery or on the Internet. It's important, though, that you have host plants already in place to provide the beneficials with food and shelter.

Happily for us, some of the good insects also have remarkably good taste, especially when it comes to herbs: basil, cilantro, dill, Florence fennel, mint, and parsley all have bug-friendly snack-size flowers. Herbs and flowers used for groundcovers, such as thyme and evening primrose, also provide handy shelter for ground beetles, which feed on many soil-inhabiting pests such as cutworms and root maggots. Try catnip, chamomile, daisy, and peppermint to attract parasitic wasps and hoverflies. The key to providing beneficials with food and shelter is to vary the heights and shapes of your host plants, since some predators, like the praying mantis, like to skulk around the stalks and leaves while trolling for victims, while others go for the easy food visible on blossoms and flowers. Think zinnias or sunflowers—both are available in varying heights, flower sizes, and colors, and a good mix of either or both will attract a variety of beneficial insects to your garden.

At the end of a growing season, let some of your lettuces or broccoli bolt and go to seed; the flowers and seeds are good beneficial bug magnets. Instead of cleaning out the garden completely, leave a few plants standing to provide food and shelter for beneficials between growing seasons, when food sources are scarce.

CROP ROTATION

The reasoning behind crop rotation is twofold: to prevent pest and disease buildup and to maintain healthy soil. A disease-causing organism, such as a fungus or bacteria, generally affects an entire plant family. Consequently, I like to plant members of a single family in the same general vicinity within a raised bed to make crop rotation easier. Once the growing season is over, all of the plants in that family are taken out of that section of the garden, thereby removing the host plants for disease-causing organisms that target that plant family. When a new family is rotated into the spot next season, that organism is not going to go after it. In essence, you starve the disease-causing organism; after one season without a host plant to feed on, it will generally die off.

By planting members of a single plant family together, I don't have to worry about disease-causing organisms being spread throughout my garden. Rather, they will be isolated in the vicinity of their host plant family. (See Chapter 5 for a list of plant families to help you group plants together.)

If you run out of space in which to rotate your plant families in your raised beds, you can also consider planting in containers to gain a little extra gardening space. If a vegetable grown in a container suffers from pests or a disease, the solution is simple: Just dispose of the entire plant in the trash, throw out all of the soil, and then scrub the pot with warm soapy water. Now the pot's safe for whatever you want to plant in it next.

Crop rotation will also ensure that vegetable families don't deplete the same nutrients from the soil year after year. So-called heavy feeders, such as leafy and fruiting crops like broccoli, lettuce, and tomatoes, tend to deplete soil nutrients—especially nitrogen—quickly. Root crops tend to be moderate feeders, while onions and garlic are light feeders. Members of the Legume family, such as beans and peas, help build up soil fertility by adding nitrogen back in.

If your initial planting was a heavy feeder (such as tomatoes), plant a moderate feeder (such as Florence fennel or parsley) in that spot the second year, and plant a light feeder (such as shallots or garlic) the third year.

Vegetables grown in containers should also be rotated to maintain healthy soil. If a plant performed well and did not have problems with pests or diseases, there is no reason to get rid of the potting soil at the end of the season, though you will want to plant members of a different plant family in it the following season.

I recommend mapping your garden each year; refer to the previous season's map at the start of each new season to avoid planting the same plant family in the same spot.

ORGANIC CONTROLS

As a last resort, some gardeners turn to organic control methods to fend off pests, though it is important to remember that any control can be indiscriminant and is as likely to kill off beneficial insects as it is pests. Sprays, dusts, soaps, oils, and powders, even when labeled organic or natural, should be used sparingly, if at all.

Insecticidal soap is effective at inhibiting a number of damaging insects, especially aphids, spider mites, and whiteflies. If caterpillars are a problem, it is possible to spray your plants with Bt (*Bacillus thuringiensis*), a bacterial pest control. If slugs or snails are a problem, you can spread bait containing iron phosphate on the surface of the soil. Pyrethrin oil is a very effective insecticide; however, it destroys many beneficial insects, including bees, and therefore should only be used as a last resort. Neem oil tends to be less toxic to many beneficial insects and is a good alternative to pyrethrin oil. Sulphur dust is used to treat powdery mildews. When applying any pesticide, it is very important to follow the label instructions.

Rather than getting in the habit of applying organic pesticides, I tell my students to focus on improving the overall growing conditions in their gardens. Perhaps the microclimate does not agree with what you're trying to grow. The stress that the plant is under from the wrong soil pH, uncomfortable temperatures, water issues, and so forth may leave it vulnerable to pests no matter how often it is sprayed with a pesticide. In other words, if the plant is not grown in optimal conditions, it will be under stress and susceptible to pests. By improving the overall growing conditions in your garden, you will reduce, if not eliminate, the need to intervene with a commercial control product.

ANIMAL PESTS

If you have animal invaders looking for food in your garden, you may have to use barriers, either under the bed (for gophers and moles) or as fences (for rabbits and woodchucks), or you may need traps. It's not really a matter of sharing a few plants with animals; if they're allowed to graze in your garden, animal pests will eventually eat everything, and sometimes they can do so overnight.

I work in an urban area, and rats are the most common (and hardest to resolve) animal pest problem my clients face. Unfortunately, their gardens represent a wonderful buffet. Rats can mow down an entire veggie bed in a night. They can chew through and climb over just about anything you throw at them, so keeping them out of the garden isn't a realistic option. If you are in an urban setting, you will have to trap them. (This is also an effective way to keep their cousin—the squirrel—at bay.) Unless you have a good local predator population of cats or dogs, you—and your trap—will have to be the predator.

If you have rabbits or woodchucks in your neighborhood, you will want to construct a 2- to 4-foot-tall fence around your garden before you plant it, so these pests have no opportunity to sample your vegetables. To prevent them from burrowing under or jumping over the fence, buy fencing 1 foot taller than you need and sink it 1 foot into the ground.

Although skunks can be highly disruptive to the garden, they aren't interested in your plants. Rather, they push them aside as they search for grubs. You can simply replant anything that has been knocked over by a skunk. Since skunks are nocturnal, they don't like bright lights. If you have lighting close to your garden, leave it on all night (or use a motion sensor).

Raccoons love corn and melons and will be attracted to your yard by a poorly maintained compost heap. Bury eggshells and produce scraps deep in the pile, and don't leave any pet food outside. Pick up any fallen fruit or nuts in your yard, and make sure your trash can has a tight-fitting lid.

Gophers, moles, and voles are voracious feeders that will go after your garden from the bottom up. More than once I've noticed a sickly looking plant that was just fine the day before, and when I gave it a tug, the entire thing came out. It was just a stalk in the ground, with no root-ball. If you know you have gophers or moles in your yard (or nearby), use a heavy-gauge wire mesh barrier to line the bottom of your raised bed before you fill it with soil. Voles are harder to deter since they attack from the top of the bed, but they can be stopped in their tracks if you set numerous snap traps (baited with peanut butter) on multiple evenings wherever voles run.

Deer are not generally considered a problem in urban Los Angeles, but they are an increasing problem in the foothills and canyons around the city and in many other regions of the country. Once they discover your garden, they'll drop by repeatedly for a nibble. Surrounding your garden with a fence will keep them out, but the fence will need to be at least 8 feet high to be effective. More practical solutions may include deer deterrents like prickly or highly scented landscape plants (such as agaves, boxwood, flowering dogwood, and Russian sage); closely planted barrier plants; and scare devices, such as motion sensors, which light up and make noise when they detect movement.

· 9 ·

CARING FOR THE GARDEN OFF-SEASON

Once September arrives, I am so sick of tomatoes that I'm glad to see them go. In summer, everything grows so quickly and the garden is thick and lush. Come fall and winter, everything slows down. It's a relief to have that break, although it does mean that beautiful and delicious bounty can be harder to come by.

The transition of your garden from summer to winter is a period of less work but more thought. It means collecting seeds, pruning perennials, composting annuals, and planning for either a winter garden or next summer's. At the end of summer, I do not take everything out at once because I have crops that are still producing. But I remove anything that is spent—my beans, cucumbers, and peppers—and top off the bed with well-finished compost, which I scatter around the still-productive plants.

And then I start to think about what I'll want to eat throughout the winter and the following year.

This last task is obviously the most important. Get into the habit of thinking a season ahead, specifically about potential menus well down the road. Do you want heirloom tomatoes for your burgers on Labor Day? Mint and oregano with your Easter lamb? Can you stretch out your salad greens until Thanksgiving or harvest short-season potatoes for New Year's? Think about what you wish you had planted this year, and make that part of next year's garden.

You could transition a garden in a single day, but why rush? Spend some time thinking about the process. This is your opportunity to ask yourself some questions and maybe start a record of what worked, what didn't, what you had too much of, and what you didn't have enough of. You'll find that you went back again and again to harvest from certain plants, while there were others you grew but didn't harvest with enthusiasm. Maybe you discovered that you actually didn't cook with sorrel or you felt that the corn took up a huge amount of space for minimal return. And what do you wish you had planted but didn't have the courage to try? What are you courageous enough to try now?

After one season, you will have figured out both what you like to eat and also what you have room for. Nobody really understands how enormous and gangly a tomato plant can become if left to its own devices. Similarly, squash can easily take over a garden, so maybe you'll want to think about planting vertically next time. One lemon cucumber vine can produce anywhere from 50 to 100 cucumbers, so growing three or four plants can result in far more cucumbers than is reasonable. You may decide to only buy one plant in the future.

Finally, take note of which plant families were planted where in your garden and how they did; you may want to keep a record from year to year, in a journal or notebook, and list which crops you planted and how they fared in a particular spot. You'll want to rotate your crops the following season, and your journal will help guide you. (For more on crop rotation, see Chapter 8.)

COOL WEATHER GROWING POSSIBILITIES

If your climate allows it, consider planting a fall lettuce crop, even while you're transitioning the garden by harvesting the last tomatoes and yanking out scraggly cucumber vines. Many salad greens can be harvested through Thanksgiving if planted in early fall.

In mild winter areas where it rarely, if ever, freezes, winter is the best time to grow broccoli rabe, Brussels sprouts, kale, potatoes, and spinach, as well as root vegetables such as carrots, parsnips, and turnips. Leeks are particularly freeze-tolerant and can be harvested well into winter. Even better, most of the common warm-weather pests and diseases either slow down or disappear completely when the weather turns cooler, making fall and winter gardening that much easier to do.

In Los Angeles, my winter garden typically includes broccoli rabe; Brussels sprouts, especially 'Rubine Red'; chervil; cilantro; lots of kale, especially Tuscan black kale ('Cavolo Nero'); leeks; butterhead lettuce; Italian parsley; shelling peas; fingerling potatoes;

savoy cabbage; spinach, especially 'Bloomsdale'; Swiss chard; and the essential perennial herbs I always have growing—oregano, rosemary, sage, savory, and thyme. I plant several winter squashes during summer, including acorn, butternut, and delicata, along with sweet potatoes, which I am then able to enjoy throughout the winter.

Garlic is an essential plant in the fall garden, regardless of where you live. Be sure to order a bulb from a specialty grower, rather than trying to plant one from the supermarket. You'll have a much larger selection of varieties to choose from and will also avoid the risk of planting cloves that have been sprayed with an antisprouting chemical. Once you have it, garlic is incredibly easy to grow. Simply separate the individual cloves and plant them in the ground, papery skins and all, letting them sit out the winter. In spring they will send out shoots, and by summer each clove will have turned into a full head of garlic. Be sure to save a few cloves to replant for your next crop.

Finally, think about vegetables that require long-range planning, such as asparagus and artichokes. These are plants that many people are afraid to grow, and they should be put into the bed in fall. Both take a long time to mature. If you grow asparagus, it can literally take years before you can harvest it, but once it's in place, you can return to it for decades with very little work on your part. Artichokes are the same way, although they do produce more rapidly—you may have a small crop within the first year. Both asparagus

---

SAVING SEEDS

Saving seeds from plants with desirable traits is a great way to grow plant varieties specifically suited to your growing conditions. You can only save seeds from plants grown from open-pollinated seeds, however, so be sure not to buy seed packets labeled "hybrid" or "F1." You will want to harvest seeds from plants that are vigorous and show no signs of disease.

Pick seedpods when they have dried out, but before they break open. Let fleshy fruits, such as melons, squash, and tomatoes, remain on the plant until they are slightly overripe, but before they begin to rot. Clean their seeds and remove as much flesh as possible by letting them sit in a jar of water for a few days. Once the seeds have sunk to the bottom of the jar and are free of all pulp, they are ready to dry.

Allow seeds to air-dry for a week—simply spread them on newspaper and set them aside in an area where they won't be damaged or blown away. Pack dry seeds in airtight jars and store them in a cool, dry place, such as the refrigerator. Seeds should be labeled with the variety name and date of harvest.

---

and artichokes have a permanent space requirement, however, and are best situated in a dedicated bed of their own.

COVER CROPS

Cover crops are great between-season crops because they require minimal effort, add nitrogen to the soil, feed the beneficial insects and microorganisms that you want to keep in your bed, and help aerate the soil with their roots. Everything they do helps prep the ground for next year's garden.

Cover crops are easy to plant, requiring nothing more than seeding and initial watering. Remove all previous crop debris and any weeds in your bed, and rake the soil surface to break up any clumps. Scatter the seeds evenly on all sides of the bed, sowing thickly. Keep the cover crop seeds watered and moist, and continue to water until the plants get to about 2 inches tall—after that, they're on their own. If possible, sow just before rain is expected. If that's not possible, water the seeds well and then cover them with a thin layer of straw or grass clippings to retain surface moisture and keep the birds from discovering the seed.

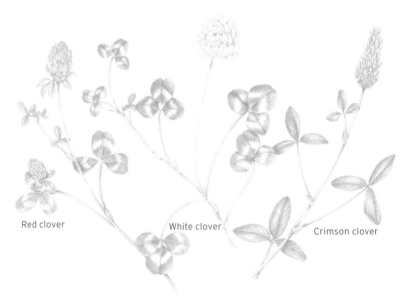

Red clover   White clover   Crimson clover

COVER CROPS. Clovers are beautiful and effective cover crops.

There are many cover crops to choose from, but I prefer crops that I can turn under easily in spring, and I especially like clovers. All clovers attract beneficial insects and enrich the soil when turned under. Red clover has deep taproots, which help improve soil drainage. Crimson clover is killed by temperatures below 0°F, making it a very easy crop to turn under in spring. White clover is a great choice for paths or as a living mulch under taller vegetables. Most clovers will survive over winter and should be planted 6 weeks before the first frost date in your area (or in fall, in mild climates).

You will want to cut down cover crops approximately 1 month before you replant the bed with vegetables, flowers, and herbs in spring. Cut off the cover crop at ground level with either pruning shears or a weed whip, and leave the cut material in place on the raised bed. The cut stems will die and dry out, adding another layer of organic material to your soil.

REPLENISHING YOUR SOIL

It doesn't matter if you're growing a winter garden or a cover crop, or simply letting the bed rest: You will still have to attend to the soil. Begin by removing all plants that suffered disease or insect problems during the summer and disposing of them in the trash. (Make sure you remove and discard their roots, too.) When removing beans and peas, cut them off at ground level, and leave the root-ball in the soil to decompose. That root-ball is what is fixing nitrogen in the soil, so it's important not to remove it. If the plants were healthy, add the stems and foliage to your compost pile.

After removing summer annuals from my garden beds and composting them, I top off the bed with additional well-finished compost to feed my winter crop. And, as always, I only lightly till this new layer of compost into the top 1 to 2 inches of soil. I also add a container of earthworms every fall: I buy my earthworms from my local nursery or bait shop (note that these are not the red wigglers used in worm bins). There are usually 50 earthworms per container, which is plenty for a 4 x 8-foot raised bed. I water the soil in the early evening and then scatter the earthworms over the surface. By morning, they've all worked their way underground.

If your bed is going to sit idle until spring without a cover crop, I suggest adding a container of earthworms, then sheet composting (adding raw organic kitchen scraps directly on top of the soil surface) to replenish the soil, and then topping it off with a 2- to 3-inch layer of leaf mulch. (See Chapter 4 for more details on sheet composting.)

If you still have plants in containers at the end of the season, move them indoors if the plants are still producing. Or, if you don't have room indoors or they have stopped producing for the season, remove the plants. Unless a container plant was diseased, you can use the soil in your containers again next season. (If you did have disease problems in your containers, discard the affected plants and the soil they grew in, and wash the pot in warm soapy water.) If you are not going to plant in the pot over winter, just top it off with a layer of leaf mulch and let it sit. Clay pots need to be stored indoors so they don't freeze and crack over winter.

ADDITIONAL END-OF-SEASON MAINTENANCE

Prune back all perennials in late fall to encourage lots of new growth in spring. Fall is also the time to divide any large perennials that threaten to take over your raised beds. In colder areas, use leaves to heavily mulch all perennials to protect them from root damage over winter.

Now make a good slow inspection of your beds. Did you have tunneling animal pests last summer? If so, this is the time to unpack the bed completely and lay down a heavy-gauge wire mesh barrier to keep them out. Is the bed's frame holding together nicely? Do you have room for an additional bed? Now is the time to make repairs as well as plans for any additional beds you may want to have ready in spring.

You'll be watering far less over winter, if at all. Now is the time to check your drip irrigation system. Flush out the drip lines and think about how the current setup worked. Did you have enough water? Too much? Consider looking into rain barrels, if you haven't already considered them, or inquire with your municipality about rainwater catchment possibilities.

Tidying up in fall makes getting your garden up and running again the next season so much easier to do. It also means your soil will remain alive and healthy and able to produce a bountiful harvest for you—and your table—each year.

· 10 ·

SEASONAL RECIPES
AND MENUS

The following recipes and menus are intended to help you enjoy the fresh flavors of your garden at their best. A few well-chosen ingredients make all the difference. Grab a basket and go into your garden. Harvest only what you can use for a single meal, selecting only the ripest vegetables growing at that moment. Let your garden be your guide—plan your meal around your vegetables and herbs. A good recipe reflects the best the season has to offer.

• STARTERS •

BAKED CANNELLINI BEANS WITH TOMATO, FETA, AND DILL PESTO

SERVES 4

2 cups dill fronds, lower stems removed	**Coarse sea salt**
1 clove garlic, cut in half	**Freshly ground black pepper**
Zest of 1 lemon	**1 can (15 ounces) cannellini beans**
1/3 cup raw sliced almonds, lightly toasted	**2 medium-size heirloom tomatoes, cut into 1/2" slices**
3-4 tablespoons extra-virgin olive oil, plus additional	**1/3 cup crumbled sheep's milk feta**
	1/2 loaf country white bread, sliced and toasted

First, make the pesto. In a food processor, combine the dill, garlic, lemon zest, and almonds. Pulse until finely chopped. With the processor running, slowly add the oil and process until well blended. The pesto should be thick, not thin. Season with salt and pepper to taste, and set aside.

Preheat the oven to 350°F.

Rinse and drain the beans, and place them in an oiled 10" ovenproof skillet. Cover the beans with a layer of tomato slices. Sprinkle with the feta and drizzle with olive oil to coat.

Bake, uncovered, until the beans are heated through and the feta is lightly browned, 20 to 30 minutes.

Remove from the oven and allow to cool for 10 minutes. Garnish with dollops of dill pesto. Serve in the skillet with slices of toasted bread.

CHILLED CUCUMBER-AVOCADO SOUP
WITH BORAGE BLOSSOMS

SERVES 4

1 ripe Haas avocado, halved and peeled

2 long green cucumbers, peeled and cut into ½" pieces

1 cup whole milk yogurt

1 cup ice water

1 handful chives, chopped

1 tablespoon fresh lemon juice, plus additional

½ teaspoon ground cumin, plus additional

Coarse sea salt

Freshly ground black pepper

24 borage blossoms

In a blender, combine the avocado, cucumbers, yogurt, water, chives, lemon juice, and cumin. Blend until very smooth, about 2 minutes. Taste. Add more lemon juice or cumin, if desired. Season with salt and pepper to taste. Chill. To serve, divide the soup among 4 bowls, and garnish each one with 6 borage blossoms.

GRILLED BROCCOLI RABE, BURRATA,
AND OREGANO PIZZA

SERVES 4

½ teaspoon active dry yeast

¾ cup warm (not hot) water

Pinch of sugar

1¾ cups all-purpose flour, plus additional for dusting

½ teaspoon coarse sea salt, plus additional

1 tablespoon extra-virgin olive oil, plus additional

2 bunches broccoli rabe

4 cloves garlic, thinly sliced

8 ounces whole milk burrata (fresh Italian cheese)

2 tablespoons dried oregano

Freshly ground black pepper

First, make the dough. In a large bowl, combine the yeast, water, and sugar, and let stand until foamy, about 5 minutes. (If bubbles do not form within 5 minutes, start over with new yeast.)

Add the flour, $\frac{1}{2}$ teaspoon of salt, and 1 tablespoon of olive oil, and stir until combined. Turn out the dough onto a lightly floured surface and knead with floured hands until smooth, about 2 minutes. Shape into a ball. Transfer the dough to a large oiled bowl and cover with a cloth. Allow it to stand in a warm (not hot) spot until the dough has doubled in size, 20 to 25 minutes.

While the dough is rising, steam the broccoli rabe until just tender, about 3 minutes. Transfer to a cutting board and chop into 2" to 3" pieces.

Preheat the grill to medium and lightly oil a baking sheet with olive oil.

Divide the dough into 4 equal pieces. On a lightly floured surface, roll out 1 piece of dough to $\frac{1}{4}$" thick and about 7" in diameter. Transfer to the oiled baking sheet. Repeat with the remaining pieces.

Brush each piece of dough with olive oil. When the grill is ready, place the dough with oiled sides down on the grill rack. Cook until the undersides are browned, 3 to 4 minutes. Flip over with tongs and, working quickly, divide the broccoli rabe, sliced garlic, and $\frac{1}{2}$" slices (or dollops) of burrata evenly among the crusts, leaving a $\frac{1}{4}$" border around each edge. Drizzle olive oil over each entire pizza, and sprinkle with the dried oregano. Grill, covered, until the undersides are golden, about 4 minutes.

Remove the pizzas from the grill, season with salt and pepper to taste, and cut into quarters. Serve immediately.

MELON AND PROSCIUTTO

SERVES 4

1 Charentais melon

8 slices prosciutto

Extra-virgin olive oil

Coarse sea salt

Freshly ground black pepper

1 handful Genovese basil, leaves cut into thin strips

Cut the melon in half and remove the seeds and the tough outer skin. Cut each half into 1/4-inch slices.

Place 2 slices of prosciutto and 4 slices of melon on each plate. Drizzle with olive oil and season with salt and pepper to taste. Garnish with the basil and serve at room temperature.

ROASTED FETA WITH HONEY AND THYME

SERVES 4

8-ounce slab sheep's milk feta

2 tablespoons extra-virgin olive oil

2 tablespoons honey

1 tablespoon chopped thyme

Freshly ground black pepper

Flat bread or country white bread, sliced and toasted

Preheat the oven to 400°F.

Place the feta in an ovenproof ceramic dish or an ovenproof skillet lined with aluminum foil. Cover with the olive oil. Bake until the cheese is soft but not melted, about 8 minutes.

Preheat the broiler.

In a small saucepan, heat the honey and thyme until just hot. Cover and remove from the heat, and let steep for 1 minute. Pour the honey mixture over the cheese. Broil until the top of the cheese browns and just starts to bubble. Season with pepper to taste. Serve immediately with slices of toasted bread.

ROASTED GARLIC

SERVES 4

2 whole garlic bulbs

6 sprigs thyme

Extra-virgin olive oil

Coarse sea salt

Freshly ground black pepper

Crusty bread, sliced and toasted

Preheat the oven to 350°F.

Slice the top ¼" to ½" off of each bulb of garlic to reveal the individual cloves within. Place the garlic heads root side down in a small ceramic baking dish, such as a ramekin. Place the thyme on top of the garlic, drizzle with olive oil, and season with salt and pepper to taste. Cover with foil and bake until very soft, about 1 hour. Remove the foil and thyme and allow to cool to room temperature. To serve, use a butter knife to scoop out the soft garlic pulp. Serve with slices of toasted bread.

ROMESCO SAUCE

MAKES ABOUT 2½ CUPS

1 large tomato

6 piquillo pimiento peppers or 2 red bell peppers

1 dried ancho chile

⅓ cup extra-virgin olive oil

3 cloves garlic

¼ teaspoon dried hot red pepper flakes

⅓ stale baguette, crusts removed and cut into ½" cubes

2 tablespoons hazelnuts, toasted and loose skins rubbed off

2 tablespoons raw almonds, toasted

1-1½ tablespoons sherry vinegar or red wine vinegar

½ teaspoon smoked Spanish paprika

¼ teaspoon fine sea salt, plus additional

Freshly ground black pepper

Baguette, toasted

Preheat the oven to 400°F. Line a rimmed baking sheet with foil.

Roast the tomato and peppers whole on a baking sheet until they're tender and the skins peel off easily, about 30 minutes. Keep the tomato and peppers separate on the pan.

While the tomato and peppers are roasting, slit the ancho chile open lengthwise, discard the stem and seeds, and tear the chile into small pieces. Heat the oil in a heavy 10" skillet over medium heat and cook the chile, stirring, until it's fragrant and it turns a brighter red, 30 seconds to 1 minute. Use a slotted spoon to transfer the chile to a bowl.

Smash the garlic. Place the garlic and red pepper flakes in the skillet and cook until just fragrant. Add the bread, hazelnuts, and almonds. Cook, stirring, until the bread and garlic are golden, 2 to 3 minutes. Pour the mixture (including the oil) into the bowl with the chile, and let cool slightly.

Peel the roasted tomato and peppers, then coarsely chop and transfer (with juices) to a blender. Add the bread and chili mixture, vinegar, paprika, and ¼ teaspoon of salt, and puree until smooth. If the sauce is very thick, thin with water. Season with additional salt and pepper to taste. Serve with toasted baguette slices.

Adapted from *The Moro Cookbook,* by Sam and Sam Clark.

SWEET CORN SOUP WITH SAGE BROWN BUTTER

SERVES 4

10 ears sweet corn, uncooked

1½ teaspoons extra-virgin olive oil

1½ teaspoons plus ½ cup unsalted butter

2 sweet onions, such as Vidalia or Maui, diced

½ teaspoon coarse sea salt, plus additional

Freshly ground black pepper

1 large fingerling potato, peeled and diced

4 cups chicken stock

16 fresh sage leaves, torn in half

Garlic bread

To make the soup: Use a large-hole grater over a very large bowl to grate off the corn kernels. Use the blunt side of a knife blade to scrape the remaining liquid and corn bits into the bowl after you grate each cob. Set aside.

In a large pot, heat the oil and 1½ teaspoons of the butter over medium heat. Add the onions and ½ teaspoon of salt. Cook, stirring occasionally, until the onions wilt, about 3 minutes. Add the potato and stock to the pot. Bring to a boil, and reduce the heat to low. Simmer until the onions and potatoes are very soft, about 10 minutes.

Add the corn. Cook until heated through, about 2 minutes. Transfer to a blender or use an immersion blender to puree until creamy and smooth. Add salt and pepper to taste. Keep warm.

To make the brown butter: Put the remaining ½ cup butter in a cold skillet and place it over medium heat. Cook, stirring occasionally to prevent it from burning (but without moving the pan), until it stops foaming and browns evenly, 3 to 4 minutes. Add the sage leaves and cook briefly, just until they crisp in the hot butter. Remove sage leaves and dry on paper towels.

Divide the soup among 4 bowls. Drizzle sage butter over the soup, and garnish with the crisped sage leaves. Serve immediately with garlic bread.

• SALADS AND DRESSINGS •

LITTLE GEM SALAD WITH SORREL DRESSING

SERVES 4

¼ cup sour cream

¼ cup plain whole milk yogurt

1 teaspoon Dijon mustard

1 clove garlic, minced

1 teaspoon red wine vinegar

2 tablespoons extra-virgin olive oil

Pinch of coarse sea salt

⅓ cup sorrel leaves, finely chopped

4 large handfuls Little Gem lettuce, torn into bite-size pieces

1 small bunch chives, roughly chopped

4 sprigs dill, roughly chopped

Freshly ground black pepper

To make the dressing: Blend the sour cream, yogurt, mustard, garlic, vinegar, olive oil, salt, and sorrel until very smooth, about 1 minute. Thin with water if it's too thick.

To make the salad: Toss the lettuce, chives, and dill with half of the dressing in a large mixing bowl; add more dressing if needed to just coat the lettuce. Season with salt and pepper. Serve immediately.

LEMON-OREGANO VINAIGRETTE

MAKES ABOUT ½ CUP

1 tablespoon fresh lemon juice

2 teaspoons red wine vinegar

1 tablespoon dried oregano

2 cloves garlic, minced

½ teaspoon coarse sea salt

Freshly ground black pepper

½ cup extra-virgin olive oil

In a small bowl, whisk together the lemon juice, vinegar, oregano, garlic, salt, and a dash of pepper. Pour in the olive oil in a single, steady stream, whisking constantly until blended.

POLE BEAN SALAD

SERVES 4

3 ears white sweet corn, uncooked

1 cup mixed cherry tomatoes, halved lengthwise

2 tablespoons chopped summer savory

Extra-virgin olive oil

Coarse sea salt

Freshly ground black pepper

3 handfuls green and yellow pole beans, cut into 2" pieces

1 handful each of Genovese basil and Purple Ruffles basil, torn into bite-size pieces

4 cups arugula, torn into bite-size pieces

Juice of half a lemon

8-ounce ball fresh buffalo mozzarella, cut into four pieces

Preheat the oven to 400°F.

Use a sharp kitchen knife to remove the kernels from the corncobs. Toss the kernels, tomatoes, and summer savory with olive oil to coat, and season with salt and pepper to taste. Spread the mixture evenly on a baking sheet, and roast uncovered in the oven until the tomatoes just begin to lose their shape, 10 to 12 minutes.

While the corn and tomatoes are roasting, boil the beans in salted water until just tender, about 5 minutes. Drain immediately.

In a large mixing bowl, combine the roasted corn and tomatoes with the beans, basil, and arugula. Drizzle with olive oil to lightly coat. Add the lemon juice and toss to coat. Season with salt and pepper to taste, and toss again.

Serve with the fresh mozzarella on the side.

RADICCHIO AND VIOLET SALAD

SERVES 4

1 head radicchio, cored and sliced into ¼" ribbons

1 head frisée, cored and torn into bite-size pieces

⅓ cup raw walnuts, lightly toasted and coarsely chopped

Balsamic vinegar

Extra-virgin olive oil

Coarse sea salt

Freshly ground black pepper

Walnut oil

⅓ cup crumbled chèvre

40 violet blossoms

In a large bowl, toss the radicchio, frisée, and walnuts.

Using a 1-to-3 vinegar-to-oil ratio, drizzle with vinegar and olive oil, and toss to combine. Season with salt and pepper to taste. Lightly drizzle with walnut oil and garnish with crumbled chèvre and violet blossoms. Serve immediately.

RAW KALE SALAD WITH HAZELNUTS, BLUE CHEESE, AND BLACK MISSION FIGS

SERVES 4

2 tablespoons red wine vinegar

½ shallot, minced

¼ teaspoon coarse sea salt, plus additional

Freshly ground black pepper

6 tablespoons extra-virgin olive oil

12 large Cavalo Nero or Tuscan Lacinato kale leaves

1 large handful flat leaf parsley, coarsely chopped

⅓ cup crumbled blue cheese

½ cup hazelnuts, toasted and coarsely chopped

8 fresh Black Mission figs, cut in half (or quartered, if very large)

First, make the vinaigrette. In a small bowl, whisk together the vinegar, shallot, 1/4 teaspoon of the salt, and a dash of pepper. Pour in the olive oil in a single, steady stream, whisking constantly until blended.

To make the salad: Trim any thick bottom stems off of the kale leaves and slice them, including the ribs, into 1/4" ribbons. In a large bowl, combine the kale, parsley, blue cheese, hazelnuts, and figs.

Toss the salad with half of the vinaigrette. Taste. Add more vinaigrette if the salad is too dry. Season with salt and pepper to taste, and toss again. Serve immediately.

RED QUINOA SALAD WITH UPLAND CRESS, ARUGULA, AVOCADO, AND PLUMS

SERVES 4

1 cup red quinoa

2 cups water

Coarse sea salt

2 large handfuls arugula, torn into bite-size pieces

2 large handfuls upland cress, torn into bite-size pieces

1 avocado, sliced into 1/4"-thick slices

2 plums, sliced into 1/4"-thick slices

Extra-virgin olive oil

Lemon

Freshly ground black pepper

To make the quinoa: Rinse the quinoa in a mesh strainer. In a medium-large pot, bring the quinoa, water, and a pinch of salt to a boil. Cover and reduce to a simmer. Cook until all of the water is absorbed, about 15 minutes. Once cooked, allow the quinoa to cool to room temperature.

To make the salad: In a large bowl, combine the cooled quinoa, arugula, upland cress, avocado, and plums. Drizzle with olive oil and a squeeze of lemon, and toss. Taste. Add more olive oil or lemon juice as desired. Season with salt and pepper to taste. Serve at room temperature.

SHAVED FENNEL SALAD WITH ARUGULA, AVOCADO, AND ALMONDS

SERVES 4

3 Florence fennel bulbs

1 handful Florence fennel fronds, torn into bite-size pieces

2 large handfuls arugula, torn into bite-size pieces

1 avocado, halved and cut into ¼" slices

⅓ cup raw sliced almonds, lightly toasted

Extra-virgin olive oil

Juice of ½ lemon

Coarse sea salt

Freshly ground pepper

Use a mandoline to slice the fennel bulbs as thinly as possible. (If a mandoline is not available, use a serrated knife.)

In a large mixing bowl, combine the sliced fennel, fennel fronds, arugula, avocado, and almonds. Drizzle with olive oil and lemon juice, and toss. Taste and add more lemon juice or olive oil, if desired. Season with salt and pepper to taste, and toss again. Serve immediately.

SPICY SLAW

SERVES 4

⅓ cup rice vinegar

2 teaspoons sugar

1 teaspoon grated fresh ginger

¼ cup grape seed oil

1 fresh serrano chile, finely chopped (for less heat, remove the seeds)

½ teaspoon coarse sea salt, plus additional

1 head savoy cabbage, cored and cut crosswise into ¼" slices

6 scallions, thinly sliced

1 large handful cilantro, coarsely chopped

1 small handful mint, coarsely chopped

½ cup shelled roasted peanuts

Juice of 1 lime

Sesame seed oil

Freshly ground black pepper

In a large bowl, whisk together the vinegar, sugar, ginger, grape seed oil, chile, and ½ teaspoon of the salt. Add the cabbage, scallions, cilantro, mint, and peanuts, and toss well. Drizzle with the lime juice and sesame seed oil. Toss again. Taste, and add more oil, if desired. Season with salt and pepper to taste. Let stand for 10 minutes to allow the flavors to develop, tossing occasionally, before serving.

SUMMER SPECIAL SALAD

SERVES 4

4 cups arugula, torn into bite-size pieces

3 or 4 lemon cucumbers, cut into quarters or bite-size cubes

½ Charentais melon, peeled, seeded, and cut into bite-size cubes

6 sprigs mint, leaves torn

⅓ cup crumbled feta

⅓ cup sliced raw almonds, lightly toasted

Extra-virgin olive oil

Juice of ½ lemon

Coarse sea salt

Freshly ground black pepper

1 handful borage blossoms

In a large mixing bowl, combine the arugula, cucumbers, melon, mint, feta, and almonds. Drizzle with olive oil and lemon juice, and toss. Taste. Add more oil, if desired. Season with salt and pepper to taste, and toss again. Garnish with borage blossoms.

WARM CHICORY SALAD WITH BACON, PEPITAS, AND SHERRY WINE VINAIGRETTE

SERVES 4

6 tablespoons extra-virgin olive oil

2 tablespoons sherry wine vinegar

½ shallot, minced

¼ teaspoon coarse sea salt, plus additional

Freshly ground black pepper

4 large handfuls baby Catalogna chicory greens, torn into bite-size pieces

4 slices bacon, cooked until crispy and crumbled into bite-size pieces

¼ cup raw pepitas, toasted

Warm the olive oil in a small saucepan until just hot. In a large bowl, whisk together the vinegar, shallot, ¼ teaspoon of the salt, and a dash of pepper. Pour in the warm olive oil in a single, steady stream, whisking constantly until blended.

Immediately toss the greens, bacon, and pepitas with half of the warm vinaigrette. The greens will wilt slightly. Taste and add more vinaigrette, if desired. Season with salt and pepper to taste, and toss again. Serve immediately.

WARM SPINACH SALAD WITH BASIL AND PINE NUTS

SERVES 4

6 large handfuls spinach, either whole baby leaves or roughly chopped large leaves

2 large handfuls Genovese basil, torn into bite-size pieces

1/2 cup extra-virgin olive oil

3 cloves garlic, thinly sliced

1/3 cup raw pine nuts

Juice and zest of 1/2 lemon

Coarse sea salt

Freshly ground black pepper

Parmigiano-Reggiano, shaved paper-thin, for garnish

In a large bowl, toss the spinach and basil.

Warm the olive oil in a medium skillet over medium heat. Add the garlic and pine nuts, and stir frequently. Once the pine nuts begin to brown, add the lemon juice and zest, and heat for 30 seconds more.

Pour the oil mixture over the greens and toss to combine. The spinach will wilt slighty. Season with salt and pepper to taste. Garnish with shaved Parmigiano-Reggiano. Serve immediately.

WATERMELON WITH FETA, CRACKED CORIANDER, AND FENNEL SEEDS

SERVES 4

1 teaspoon coriander seeds, lightly toasted

1 teaspoon fennel seeds, lightly toasted

1 Sugar Baby watermelon, chilled, rind removed, and flesh cut into bite-size pieces

1/2 cup crumbled sheep's milk feta, at room temperature

Lightly pound the coriander and fennel seeds in a mortar and pestle until they're roughly cracked.

Divide the watermelon among 4 shallow bowls. Sprinkle the feta, coriander, and fennel over the melon. Serve immediately.

• MAIN COURSES •

BLOSSOM FRITTATA

SERVES 4

8 eggs

¾ cup crumbled sheep's milk feta

1 handful marjoram, leaves finely chopped

Coarse sea salt

Freshly ground black pepper

2 teaspoons extra-virgin olive oil

24 nasturtium blossoms

Preheat the oven to 425°F.

In a medium bowl, whisk together the eggs, feta, and marjoram. Season with salt and pepper to taste.

Warm the oil in a 10" ovenproof skillet over medium heat. Add the egg mixture and reduce the heat to medium-low. Cook until the frittata begins to set, 2 to 3 minutes.

Arrange the nasturtium blossoms over the surface of the frittata, completely covering it. Continue to cook until just the very top of the frittata is still soft, about 8 minutes.

Transfer the skillet to the oven. Cook until the top is golden brown and set, about 2 minutes.

Remove the frittata from the oven and allow it to cool in the pan on a rack for 1 minute. Slide the frittata onto a large platter, blossoms side up. Serve immediately.

Adapted from *A Year in a Vegetarian Kitchen*, by Jack Bishop

CHICKPEAS WITH TOMATOES, FETA, AND HERBS

SERVES 4

8 tablespoons extra-virgin olive oil, plus additional

3 cups mixed cherry tomatoes, halved

Coarse sea salt

Freshly ground black pepper

1 handful mint, coarsely chopped

1 handful flat leaf parsley, coarsely chopped

1 handful cilantro, coarsely chopped

2 cloves garlic, minced

1 can (15½ ounces) chickpeas, drained, rinsed, and patted dry

½ cup crumbled sheep's milk feta

Heat 2 tablespoons of the olive oil in a medium skillet over medium-high heat. Add the tomatoes, season with salt and pepper to taste, and cook until barely soft, about 2 minutes. Remove from the pan. In a large bowl, combine the lightly sautéed tomatoes, mint, parsley, cilantro, garlic, and 4 tablespoons of the olive oil. Season with salt and pepper to taste.

Heat the remaining 2 tablespoons of the olive oil in the same pan used for cooking the tomatoes over medium-high heat. Add the chickpeas and cook until lightly browned, about 5 minutes.

Add the chickpeas to the tomato mixture and toss to coat. Add the feta and toss again. Taste. Drizzle with olive oil if dry. Season with salt and pepper to taste. Serve warm or at room temperature.

FINES HERBES OMELET

SERVES 2

5 eggs

Coarse sea salt

Freshly ground black pepper

1 teaspoon olive oil

1 teaspoon unsalted butter

⅓ cup lightly chopped fresh herbs, such as parsley, tarragon, chives, and chervil

Beat the eggs thoroughly. Add a pinch of salt and a generous twist of pepper.

Heat the olive oil and butter in a 10" omelet pan over medium heat. Add the eggs. Gently stir with a heatproof spatula for 1 to 2 minutes, to create small curds. When most of the mixture is solid, add the chopped herbs and cook without stirring for 30 seconds. (This will create a thin solid layer on the underside of the mixture, binding it together.)

Using a spatula, fold the omelet in half, slide it from the pan onto a plate, and cut it in half. Season with salt and pepper to taste.

GRILLED FLANK STEAK WITH CHIMICHURRI

SERVES 4

1 large clove garlic

1½ cups fresh cilantro

1½ cups fresh flat leaf parsley

¼ cup distilled white vinegar

⅓ cup olive oil

¼ teaspoon cayenne

1½ teaspoons coarse sea salt

1½ pounds trimmed flank steak

½ teaspoon ground cumin

½ teaspoon ground coriander

¼ teaspoon freshly ground black pepper

Preheat the grill. (The steak can also be prepared in the broiler, if a grill is not available.)

To make the chimichurri sauce: In a food processor, combine the garlic, cilantro, parsley, vinegar, oil, cayenne, and ½ teaspoon of the salt. Process until the herbs are finely chopped.

To make the steak: Pat the steak dry. In a small bowl, combine the cumin, coriander, pepper, and the remaining 1 teaspoon of the salt, and rub the mixture onto both sides of the steak.

Grill the steak for 6 minutes per side, or until a thermometer inserted in the center registers 135°F for medium-rare. (Or broil the steak on a broiler pan about 4" from the heat for 6 minutes per side.) Transfer the steak to a cutting board, and let it stand for 5 minutes.

Thinly slice the steak. Serve immediately with the chimichurri sauce.

LAMB CHOPS WITH CILANTRO-MINT YOGURT DRESSING

SERVES 4

12 lamb chops*

6 cloves garlic, crushed with the side of a knife

1 tablespoon extra-virgin olive oil, plus additional

1 bunch fresh mint leaves

1 bunch fresh cilantro leaves

1 cup plain whole milk yogurt

¼ teaspoon coarse sea salt, plus additional

Freshly ground black pepper

Place the lamb chops in a single layer in a shallow dish. Add the garlic, getting some on each chop. Drizzle with enough olive oil to lightly coat the chops. Toss to coat both sides, then cover with plastic wrap and refrigerate for at least 8 hours. Remove from the fridge 1 hour before cooking.

In a blender, combine the mint, cilantro, yogurt, 1 tablespoon of olive oil, and ¼ teaspoon of salt. Blend until completely smooth. Pour into a bowl, cover with plastic wrap, and refrigerate until an hour before cooking.

An hour before cooking, set out the chops and yogurt sauce to bring them to room temperature. Preheat a grill or broiler to medium-high.

*Have the butcher "French" the rib chops, that is, scrape the top portions of the bones clean.

Season the chops with salt and pepper to taste on both sides. Grill or broil the chops for 5 minutes, turning once, or until browned and a thermometer inserted in the center registers 135°F for medium-rare.

Arrange the chops on a warm serving platter and drizzle with the yogurt sauce. Serve immediately.

LINGUINE WITH ARUGULA PECAN PESTO

SERVES 4

³⁄₄ cup pecans, lightly toasted

1 clove garlic

4 cups arugula, washed and stems removed

¹⁄₂ cup finely grated Parmigiano-Reggiano

¹⁄₂ cup extra-virgin olive oil

¹⁄₂ teaspoon coarse sea salt

¹⁄₂ teaspoon freshly ground black pepper

1 pound dried linguine

Finely chop ¼ cup of the pecans with a knife and set aside.

In a food processor, combine the garlic, arugula, Parmigiano-Reggiano, oil, salt, pepper, and ½ cup of the pecans. Process until smooth, 1 to 2 minutes. Cook the pasta in salted boiling water until al dente, about 10 minutes. Ladle out and set aside 1 cup of the pasta cooking water. Drain the pasta and return it to the pot.

Combine the pasta, pesto, and reserved cooking water. Divide between 4 bowls and garnish with the remaining chopped pecans. Serve immediately.

ROASTED CHICKEN SALAD WITH CELERY, HERBS, AND CROUTONS

SERVES 4

12 tablespoons extra-virgin olive oil

4 cups 1" bread cubes

3 cups pulled roasted chicken, at room temperature

⅓ cup sliced raw almonds, lightly toasted

2 large handfuls upland cress, torn into bite-size pieces

2 large handfuls frisée, torn into bite-size pieces

2 stalks celery, sliced into ¼" pieces

1 handful tarragon, coarsely chopped

1 handful flat leaf parsley, stems removed and coarsely chopped

1 handful dill, stems removed and coarsely chopped

2 tablespoons cider vinegar

½ shallot, minced

¼ teaspoon coarse sea salt, plus additional

Dash freshly ground black pepper, plus additional

To make the croutons: Heat 6 tablespoons of the olive oil in a large skillet over medium heat. Add the bread cubes and toss to coat. (The bread cubes should be in a single layer; if the pan is not large enough to accommodate all the cubes at once in a single layer, cook in batches.) Stir regularly until the bread cubes are golden brown and slightly crispy. Remove from the pan and cool on paper towels.

In a large mixing bowl, combine the croutons, chicken, almonds, upland cress, frisée, celery, tarragon, parsley, and dill.

To make the vinaigrette: Whisk together the vinegar, shallot, ¼ teaspoon of salt, and dash of pepper. Pour in the remaining 6 tablespoons of olive oil in a single, steady stream, whisking constantly until blended.

Toss the chicken salad with the vinaigrette. Season with salt and pepper to taste, and toss again. Serve immediately.

ROAST CHICKEN WITH SAVORY

SERVES 4

1 chicken (5 pounds), washed and patted dry

1 large handful winter savory

1 head garlic, cut in half lengthwise

Extra-virgin olive oil

Coarse sea salt

Freshly ground black pepper

Preheat the oven to 425°F.

Stuff the chicken with savory and garlic. (The entire cavity should be filled, though savory should not stick out.) Place the chicken breast side up on a roasting rack in a baking pan. Rub the exterior of the chicken with enough olive oil to coat, and sprinkle it with salt and pepper to taste.

Roast for 1 to 1½ hours, or until a meat thermometer inserted into the thigh reads 170°F. Remove the chicken from the oven, lightly cover it with foil, and allow it to rest on its rack for 5 minutes. Transfer the chicken to a cutting board and cut into 8 to 10 pieces. Serve immediately.

• SIDES •

BASMATI RICE WITH SPICES, PISTACHIOS, AND CALENDULA

SERVES 4

1 tablespoon fine sea salt

2 cups basmati rice, washed and drained

4 tablespoons unsalted butter

2 tablespoons cumin seeds

2 tablespoons coriander seeds

1 cup calendula petals

1½ cups shelled raw pistachios, coarsely chopped

Bring 2 quarts of water and the salt to a boil in a 4-quart pot. Parboil the rice, uncovered, for 15 minutes. Drain in a large mesh strainer.

Clean the pot, and melt the butter in it over low heat. Add the cumin and coriander, and cook for 1 minute. Remove the pan from the heat.

Spoon the parboiled rice into the pan, alternating with sprinklings of calendula petals and pistachios, and ending with rice. Use the round handle of a wooden spoon to make 5 or 6 holes in the rice right to the bottom of the pot, then cover. Cook the rice, undisturbed, over low heat until it's tender and a crust forms on the bottom, 30 to 35 minutes. Stir to combine, including the crispy bits from the bottom of the pan. Serve immediately.

BRAISED BABY ARTICHOKES

SERVES 4

20-24 whole baby artichokes

3 tablespoons extra-virgin olive oil

4 cloves garlic, smashed

½ cup dry white wine

Zest of 1 lemon

1 handful flat leaf parsley, roughly chopped

1 handful mint, roughly chopped

Coarse sea salt

Freshly ground black pepper

Remove all of the tough outer leaves of the baby artichokes, down to the tender pale leaves in the center. Cut off any remaining thorns on the tips of the leaves, and halve lengthwise.

Heat the oil in a large skillet over medium heat. (Use a skillet large enough for the artichoke halves to cook in a single layer.) Add the garlic. As soon as the garlic is fragrant (30 to 45 seconds), add the artichokes, toss to coat with the olive oil, and then position the halves in a single layer.

Sauté until the artichokes begin to color, 2 to 3 minutes, then add the wine. When the wine boils off, add 1 cup of water and the lemon zest, cover, and reduce the heat to low. Cook until the artichokes are tender, 8 to 10 minutes, stirring occasionally to prevent the artichokes from sticking to the pan. Once tender (if a fork easily pierces the artichokes, they're tender and are done cooking), toss with the parsley and mint and immediately cover again. Turn off the heat and allow to sit, covered, for 1 minute. Season with salt and pepper to taste. Serve while still warm.

BRAISED BRUSSELS SPROUTS WITH BACON, GARLIC, AND CIDER VINEGAR

SERVES 4

1 pound small Brussels sprouts, trimmed and halved lengthwise

1/4 pound bacon, cut crosswise into 1/2" strips

2 cloves garlic, minced

1/2 tablespoon extra-virgin olive oil

Coarse sea salt

Freshly ground black pepper

1/4 cup cider vinegar

Preheat the oven to 450°F.

In an 11" x 7" baking pan or on a rimmed baking sheet, toss together the Brussels sprouts, bacon, garlic, and oil. Add salt and pepper to taste, and toss again. Spread in a single layer.

Roast in the upper third of the oven for about 25 minutes, or until the sprouts are tender and brown on the edges. Stir once halfway through roasting to prevent sprouts from sticking to the pan. Once they are tender and brown, stir in the vinegar, scraping up the brown bits. Continue to cook for 2 or 3 minutes more. Remove from oven and season with salt and pepper to taste. Serve warm.

BRAISED LEEKS

SERVES 4

6 tablespoons butter

6-8 large leeks, trimmed and cleaned,
cut into 16 sections 4" long

Coarse sea salt

Freshly ground black pepper

2 cups chicken stock

8 sprigs thyme

½ lemon

Heat the butter in a large skillet over medium heat. When the butter melts, add
the leeks in a single layer. (If the pan is not large enough to accommodate the
leeks in a single layer, cook in more than one pan.) Lightly sprinkle with salt and
pepper, and cook until the leeks just begin to color, about 5 minutes.

Add the chicken stock and thyme, and bring to a boil. Turn the heat to low, cover,
and cook until very tender, about 20 minutes. If there is still a significant amount
of chicken stock left in the pan once the leeks are tender, remove the lid, raise the
heat to medium-high, and allow most of it to cook off.

Remove the thyme. Squeeze the lemon over the leeks and stir. Season with salt
and pepper to taste. Serve immediately.

BRAISED RAINBOW CHARD ON TOAST

SERVES 4

24 large rainbow chard leaves, thick
stems removed

4 cloves garlic

4 tablespoons extra-virgin olive oil,
plus additional

2-3 cups chicken stock

Coarse sea salt

Freshly ground black pepper

½ loaf of country white bread

1 large heirloom tomato

½ lemon

Cut the chard leaves into 1"-thick ribbons and thoroughly wet them. Smash the
garlic cloves with the side of a knife. Heat the oil in a large skillet over medium
heat, add the garlic, and cook for 30 seconds, until just fragrant. Add the wet

chard. When the chard has cooked down enough to cover the pan with a lid, add the chicken stock 1 cup at a time. Continue adding stock until the chard is just covered. Simmer, uncovered, for 30 minutes, or until the stock has been completely cooked down. Season with salt and pepper to taste.

Slice and toast the bread. While the bread is toasting, slice the tomato. Pile braised chard on the toast, squeeze a bit of fresh lemon juice over it, and top with a slice of tomato. Drizzle with olive oil and sprinkle with salt.

BRAISED ROMANO BEANS WITH TOMATO AND PRESERVED LEMON

SERVES 4

2-3 tablespoons extra-virgin olive oil

2 cloves garlic, peeled and crushed with the side of a knife

4 large handfuls Romano beans (about 1 pound), trimmed

2 large heirloom tomatoes, diced into medium-size pieces, juice reserved

½ preserved lemon*, diced into medium-size pieces

Coarse sea salt

Freshly ground black pepper

1 handful flat leaf parsley, roughly chopped

Heat the olive oil in a large skillet over medium heat. Add the garlic. Add the beans as soon as you can smell the garlic. Stir to coat, and sauté for 2 to 3 minutes. Add the tomatoes, their juice, and the preserved lemon. Stir to combine, and cover. Reduce the heat to low and simmer until the beans are very tender, about 30 minutes. Season with salt and pepper to taste. Garnish with the chopped parsley.

*To make preserved lemons: Quarter whole lemons and put them in a bowl with the juice of another lemon or two. Sprinkle with a fair amount of sea salt, cover with a towel or plastic wrap, and let sit for an hour or so, until the rind begins to soften.

Adapted from Suzanne Goin, Lucques Restaurant.

EGGPLANT WITH HERBED BREAD CRUMBS AND PINE NUTS

SERVES 4

2 cloves garlic, minced

1 handful flat leaf parsley, finely chopped

1 handful basil, finely chopped

1 cup coarse bread crumbs, toasted (country white and kalamata olive bread make great bread crumbs)

¼ cup raw pine nuts, lightly toasted

⅓ cup extra-virgin olive oil, plus additional

Coarse sea salt

Freshly ground black pepper

4 long purple eggplants

In a bowl, combine the garlic, parsley, basil, bread crumbs, pine nuts, and 2 tablespoons of the olive oil. Season with salt and pepper to taste.

Cut the green tops off the eggplants and halve lengthwise. Deeply score the eggplant flesh in a crosshatched pattern, being careful not to pierce the skin at the bottom.

Spoon the herbed bread crumb mixture over the eggplant halves, firmly pressing it into the cuts.

Arrange the stuffed eggplants in a single layer, skin side down, in a large skillet. (If the pan is not large enough to accommodate the eggplants in a single layer, cook in more than one pan.) Pour the remaining olive oil over the eggplants. Cover, turn the heat to medium-low, and cook until tender, 20 to 25 minutes. Once cooked, drizzle with olive oil and season with salt and pepper to taste. Serve immediately.

Adapted from *Essentials of Classic Italian Cooking,* by Marcella Hazan.

FINGERLING POTATOES WITH CHIVE OIL

SERVES 4

1 large bunch chives

½ cup extra-virgin olive oil

1 pound fingerling potatoes, cut into 1" chunks

Fine sea salt

Freshly ground black pepper

First, make the chive oil (must be done at least 1 day in advance): Blanch the chives in boiling water for 10 seconds. Immediately move the chives to a mesh strainer and place under cold running water to stop the cooking. Roughly chop the blanched chives and, using a blender, blend with the olive oil until smooth, about 2 minutes.

Transfer the chive oil to a bowl, cover, and chill overnight. The next day, bring the oil to room temperature and pour it through a fine mesh strainer, pressing hard on the chive pieces.

Chive oil will keep for up to 1 week in the refrigerator. Always bring it to room temperature before using.

To make the potatoes: Place the potatoes in a 4-quart pan and add cold water to cover. Add a generous amount of salt to the water (it should taste salty), and bring to a boil uncovered. Simmer until the potatoes are tender, approximately 8 minutes. Drain.

Transfer the potatoes to a large bowl. Drizzle with chive oil until lightly coated—not drenched—and stir with a wooden spoon. Cover with plastic wrap and let sit for 5 minutes to allow the flavors to develop. Season with salt and pepper to taste. Serve immediately.

HEIRLOOM TOMATOES WITH WARM BUTTER AND THYME

SERVES 4

¼ cup unsalted butter

Coarse sea salt

1 tablespoon chopped thyme

Freshly cracked black pepper

3 large heirloom tomatoes, cut into
½"-thick slices

Warm the butter in a medium skillet over medium heat. Add the thyme and cook for 1 minute. Add the tomatoes, toss to coat, and increase the heat to medium-high. Cook until the tomatoes are just soft, about 2 minutes. Season with salt and pepper to taste. Serve immediately.

MUSTARD GREENS WITH CUMIN SEEDS

SERVES 4

3 tablespoons extra-virgin olive oil

2 large bunches mustard green leaves,
coarsely chopped

1 medium red onion, julienned

4 cloves garlic, smashed

1 tablespoon red wine vinegar

1 tablespoon cumin seeds

Coarse sea salt

1 teaspoon red pepper flakes

Freshly ground black pepper

Heat the oil in a large deep skillet over medium heat. Add the onion and cook until soft, about 5 minutes. Stir in the garlic, cumin seeds, and red pepper flakes. Cook for 2 minutes, stirring frequently to avoid burning.

Add the mustard greens and combine well. Reduce the heat to medium-low, cover, and cook until the greens are very tender, stirring frequently, about 30 minutes. Once the greens are tender, mix in the vinegar. Season with salt and pepper to taste. Serve immediately.

PEAS WITH BACON, SHALLOTS, BUTTER, AND DILL

SERVES 4

4 thick bacon slices, cut crosswise into ¼" pieces

2 shallots, chopped

3 cups freshly shelled peas

¾ cup water

¼ cup chopped fresh dill

Coarse sea salt

Freshly ground black pepper

2 tablespoons unsalted butter

Cook the bacon in a large skillet over medium heat, stirring occasionally until browned, about 5 minutes. Remove the bacon from the pan and pour off most of the fat from the skillet, then add the shallots and cook, stirring frequently, until they begin to soften, about 3 minutes.

Add the peas, water, half of the dill, and salt and pepper to taste. Cover and cook, stirring occasionally, until the peas are tender, about 8 minutes. Stir in the butter, bacon, and the remaining dill. Taste, and add more salt and pepper, if desired. Serve immediately.

ROASTED ASPARAGUS

SERVES 4

40-48 asparagus spears

¼ cup extra-virgin olive oil

Coarse sea salt

Freshly ground black pepper

¼ pound shaved Parmigiano-Reggiano

Balsamic vinegar

Preheat the oven to 425°F.

Wash and trim the asparagus spears. Place them in a single layer on a rimmed baking sheet and drizzle with the olive oil, a pinch or two of salt, and lots of black pepper.

Roast for 15 to 20 minutes, turning with tongs every 5 minutes or so, until the asparagus is tender and only slightly charred.

Remove from the oven and place on a serving platter or individual plates. Sprinkle Parmigiano-Reggiano on top of the asparagus and drizzle with balsamic vinegar and a little more olive oil, salt, and pepper. Serve immediately.

ROASTED POTATOES AND FENNEL
WITH NIÇOISE OLIVES

SERVES 4

1 pound fingerling potatoes, quartered

Extra-virgin olive oil

8 Florence fennel bulbs, quartered

Coarse sea salt

⅓ cup Niçoise olives, pitted

Freshly ground black pepper

1 teaspoon fennel seeds

Heat the oven to 350°F.

In a large mixing bowl, toss the potatoes, fennel, olives, and fennel seeds with enough olive oil to nicely coat all of the ingredients. Season with salt and pepper to taste.

Pour the mixture into a shallow baking dish, cover with foil, and bake until the potatoes are tender, 45 to 60 minutes. Remove the foil and continue to bake until the potatoes and fennel are lightly browned, about 10 minutes. Drizzle lightly with olive oil and serve immediately.

SAUTÉED CHERRY TOMATOES WITH MARJORAM

SERVES 4

3 tablespoons unsalted butter

3 cups mixed cherry tomatoes, halved

1 clove garlic, minced

Coarse sea salt

1 handful marjoram, stems removed and finely chopped

Freshly ground black pepper

Warm the butter in a medium skillet over medium heat. Once it's melted, add the garlic and marjoram. As soon as they're fragrant (30 to 45 seconds), add the tomatoes. Stir frequently until the tomatoes begin to soften. Remove from the heat before the tomatoes completely lose their shape, which happens in 2 to 3 minutes. Season with salt and pepper to taste. Serve immediately.

SQUASH BLOSSOMS WITH RICOTTA, MINT, AND PEPITAS

SERVES 4

Butter, to grease baking sheet

4 ounces fresh whole milk ricotta

¼ cup mint, finely chopped

⅓ cup raw pepitas, lightly toasted

Coarse sea salt

Freshly ground black pepper

16 squash blossoms, stems trimmed to ½"

1 whole egg, beaten with 1 tablespoon of water

2 cups dried fine bread crumbs

Preheat the oven to 350°F. Coat a rimmed baking sheet with butter.

In a bowl, combine the cheese, mint, and pepitas. Season with salt and pepper to taste. Use a teaspoon to stuff the squash blossoms about half-full with the cheese mixture. Twist the ends of the petals gently, and fold under to close.

Brush each stuffed blossom with the egg wash. On a rimmed baking sheet, spread the bread crumbs in an even layer. Roll each blossom in the bread crumbs and place on the buttered baking sheet.

Bake until lightly browned and crisp, about 15 minutes. Season with salt and pepper to taste. Serve immediately.

• DESSERTS •

BLACKBERRY AND LEMON THYME SORBET

MAKES ABOUT 1 QUART

4 cups blackberries

1 cup water

²/₃ cup sugar

1 teaspoon freshly squeezed lemon juice

1 tablespoon lemon thyme, chopped

In a blender, puree the blackberries with the water and sugar. Stir in the lemon juice and lemon thyme. Pour into a saucepan and warm until just hot. Remove from the heat.

Cover with plastic wrap and chill the mixture for at least 3 hours or as long as overnight.

Strain the mixture through a fine mesh sieve, then freeze in your ice cream maker according to the manufacturer's instructions.

CHARENTAIS MELON IN COCONUT MILK

SERVES 4

1 can unsweetened full-fat coconut milk

1 teaspoon fresh lime juice

2 tablespoons sugar

1 medium-size Charentais melon, chilled

Zest from 1 lime

In a metal bowl, combine the coconut milk, lime juice, and sugar until the sugar is dissolved. Cover and place in the refrigerator for 10 minutes.

Halve the melon and scoop into balls with a melon baller.

Divide the melon balls among 4 serving dishes and pour the chilled coconut milk on top. Sprinkle with the lime zest. Serve immediately.

FRESH MINT ICE CREAM

MAKES ABOUT 1 QUART

2 cups heavy whipping cream	**2 cups fresh mint leaves**
1 cup half-and-half	**3 egg yolks**
¾ cup sugar	**Pinch of salt**

Warm the cream, half-and-half, sugar, and mint in a saucepan over medium heat. Cover, remove from the heat, and steep at room temperature for 1 hour.

Strain the cream mixture through a fine mesh sieve, pressing on the mint leaves to extract as much of the flavor as possible. Discard the strained mint leaves. Return the cream mixture to the saucepan and warm it until just hot.

Whisk the egg yolks and salt in a large, heatproof bowl. Slowly pour the warm cream mixture into the egg yolks, whisking constantly, then pour the entire mixture back into the saucepan.

Stir the mixture constantly over medium heat, scraping the bottom as you stir, until it thickens and coats the back of a wooden spoon.

Strain through a fine mesh sieve, cover with plastic wrap, and cool in the refrigerator for at least 3 hours or as long as overnight.

Freeze the mixture in your ice cream maker according to the manufacturer's instructions.

LAVENDER AND HONEY ICE CREAM

MAKES ABOUT 1 QUART

2 cups heavy whipping cream	**2 tablespoons lavender flower buds**
1 cup half-and-half	**3 large egg yolks**
⅔ cup clover or other lightly flavored honey	**⅛ teaspoon salt**

Warm the cream, half-and-half, honey, and lavender in a saucepan over medium heat. Cover, remove from the heat, and steep for 30 minutes.

Strain the mixture through a fine mesh sieve, return it to the saucepan, and warm until just hot.

Whisk the egg yolks and salt in a large, heat-proof bowl. Slowly pour the warm cream mixture into the egg yolks, whisking constantly, then pour the entire mixture back into the saucepan.

Stir the mixture constantly over medium heat, scraping the bottom as you stir, until it thickens and coats the back of a wooden spoon.

Strain through a fine mesh sieve, cover with plastic wrap, and cool in the refrigerator for at least 3 hours or as long as overnight.

Freeze the mixture in your ice cream maker according to the manufacturer's instructions.

PLUM BASIL GALETTE

SERVES 4

1¼ cups all-purpose flour

⅓ cup fine yellow cornmeal

1 teaspoon sugar, plus additional

1¼ teaspoons fine sea salt

1½ tablespoons unsalted butter, chilled and cut into small cubes

3 tablespoons extra-virgin olive oil

3 tablespoons ice water

10-12 ripe plums, halved, pitted, and cut into ¼" slices, juice reserved

1 handful basil, leaves cut into thin ribbons

First, make the galette dough: In a bowl, combine the flour, cornmeal, sugar, and salt. Add the butter and blend with your fingertips until the mixture resembles wet sand. Drizzle the olive oil and ice water evenly over the mixture and stir with a fork until incorporated.

Turn out the dough onto a smooth, lightly floured work surface. Divide the dough in half and use the heel of your hand to smear each half a couple of times to distribute the butter. Gather both pieces of dough together, gently press them into a ball, and flatten the ball into a $\frac{1}{2}$"-thick disk.

Wrap the disk in plastic wrap and refrigerate until firm, for at least 1 hour or as long as overnight.

In a bowl, combine the sliced plums and basil. Dust with sugar and stir. Cover with plastic wrap and let the mixture sit for 1 hour.

When you're ready to make the galette, preheat the oven to 350°F. Line a baking sheet with parchment paper.

Working on a smooth, lightly floured work surface, roll out the dough into an 8" x 12" rectangle. Transfer to the baking sheet. Chill in the refrigerator for 5 minutes.

Working quickly, arrange the plum slices on the dough, overlapping them slightly in lengthwise rows and leaving a 1" border. Drizzle the juice from the plums over the fruit slices. Fold the border inward, covering the outer edges of the plums.

Bake the galette for 30 minutes, then cover it loosely with foil and bake for another 25 minutes, or until the filling is bubbling and the crust is golden.

Allow to cool for 10 minutes on the sheet on a rack, then remove to the rack and cool completely. Serve with vanilla ice cream or crème fraîche.

ROASTED PEACHES WITH CINNAMON BASIL SOUR CREAM

SERVES 4

1 tablespoon chopped fresh cinnamon basil

Pinch sugar

1 cup sour cream

3 tablespoons unsalted butter, softened

3 tablespoons dark brown sugar

Pinch ground cinnamon

Coarse sea salt

4 ripe peaches, halved and pitted

Preheat the oven to 375°F.

To make the sour cream (must be done at least 8 hours in advance): In a bowl, combine the basil, sugar, and sour cream until smooth. Cover with plastic wrap and refrigerate until 1 hour before serving.

To make the peach filling: In a bowl, combine the butter, brown sugar, cinnamon, and salt until smooth.

Spoon the filling into the cavities of the peach halves, and arrange the halves stuffed side up on a rimmed baking sheet. Bake until the peaches are softened and the butter is bubbling, about 20 minutes. Serve hot, warm, or at room temperature, with the cinnamon basil sour cream.

ROSEMARY BROWN SUGAR BUTTER COOKIES

MAKES ABOUT 12 SQUARES

½ cup unsalted butter, at room temperature

⅓ cup light brown sugar

¼ teaspoon salt

1 teaspoon pure vanilla extract

¾ cup + 2 tablespoons all-purpose flour

1 teaspoon rosemary, finely chopped

3 tablespoons cornstarch

Coarse sea salt

Preheat the oven to 325°F. Arrange an oven rack in the lower half of the oven.

In a large mixing bowl, use an electric mixer to combine the butter, sugar, salt, and vanilla until light and fluffy, 1 to 2 minutes.

Stir in the flour, rosemary, and cornstarch until the mixture is fairly uniform. Gather the dough into a rough ball, kneading it a few times to keep it together.

Press the dough evenly into an 8" x 8" baking dish. Prick the dough with the tines of a fork. Freeze the dough in the dish for 15 minutes. Remove from the freezer and quickly sprinkle the entire surface with coarse sea salt to cover lightly.

Bake until the edges are lightly colored and the center is no longer puffy, 30 to 35 minutes. Cool in the pan on a rack for 5 minutes. Use a sharp knife to carefully cut the cookies into squares, and remove them from the pan. Continue to cool on the rack. Serve at room temperature.

Adapted from *The Improvisational Cook,* by Sally Schneider

SAGE CORN BREAD PUDDING

SERVES 4

3 tablespoons unsalted butter, plus additional to grease pan

1½ cups yellow cornmeal

1 cup all-purpose flour

1 tablespoon baking powder

1 teaspoon fine sea salt, plus additional

3 cups whole milk

4 eggs

4 tablespoons molasses

2 tablespoons fresh sage, finely chopped

Preheat the oven to 425°F and grease an 8" x 8" baking dish with butter.

First, make the corn bread: Melt the butter and let it cool. In a large bowl, sift together the cornmeal, flour, baking powder, and 1 teaspoon of salt. In a separate bowl, whisk together the butter, 1 cup of the milk, and 1 egg, and stir into the cornmeal mixture until just combined.

Pour the batter into the baking pan and bake until the top is pale gold and a tester comes out clean, about 20 minutes. Cool the corn bread in the baking dish on a rack for 5 minutes. Invert the corn bread onto the rack and cool completely.

Reheat the oven to 275°F. Clean the dish you baked the corn bread in, and grease it with butter.

Cut the corn bread into ½" cubes and place them in the greased dish. Whisk together the remaining 2 cups of milk and 3 eggs. Whisk in the molasses, sage, and a pinch of salt. Pour over the corn bread cubes. Let stand 5 minutes.

Set the pan on a rimmed baking sheet and bake until just set, about 45 minutes. Serve warm with vanilla ice cream or heavy cream.

STRAWBERRIES AND TARRAGON CREAM

SERVES 4

2 cups heavy whipping cream

2 tablespoons lightly chopped tarragon

½ teaspoon sugar

3 cups perfectly ripe, sweet strawberries, hulled and cut into bite-size pieces

4 sprigs tarragon for garnish

Combine the cream, chopped tarragon, and sugar. Cover with plastic wrap and refrigerate for at least 8 hours. Remove from the fridge 1 hour before serving.

Divide the strawberries among 4 small bowls. Strain the cream through a fine mesh sieve and pour over the strawberries to cover. Garnish with the fresh sprigs of tarragon.

SEASONAL MENUS

A seasonal menu allows you to look around your garden for inspiration and to cook with ingredients at their prime. Your menu should not only feature the best your garden has to offer, it should also be an exploration of flavors and textures. (Think cooling watermelon with salty feta and cracked coriander.) There should be nothing too heavy or too light or too sweet; it should all work in balance, just as it works in your garden.

Dinner for a Hot Night

Melon and Prosciutto, *page 137*
Linguine with Arugula Pecan Pesto, *page 153*
Little Gem Salad with Sorrel Dressing, *page 141*
Lavender and Honey Ice Cream, *page 167*

Garden Lunch

Roasted Feta with Honey and Thyme, *page 137*
Roasted Chicken Salad with Celery, Herbs, and Croutons, *page 154*
Blackberry and Lemon Thyme Sorbet, *page 166*

Indian Summer

Watermelon with Feta, Cracked Coriander, and Fennel Seeds, *page 148*
Warm Chicory Salad with Bacon, Pepitas, and Sherry Wine Vinaigrette, *page 147*
Sweet Corn Soup with Sage Brown Butter, *page 140*
Rosemary Brown Sugar Butter Cookies, *page 170*

Sunday Steak Dinner

Grilled Flank Steak with Chimichurri, *page 151*
Heirloom Tomatoes with Warm Butter and Thyme, *page 162*
Shaved Fennel Salad with Arugula, Avocado, and Almonds, *page 145*
Sage Corn Bread Pudding, *page 171*

Savory Chicken Dinner

Raw Kale Salad with Hazelnuts, Blue Cheese, and Black Mission Figs, *page 143*
Roast Chicken with Savory, *page 155*
Fingerling Potatoes with Chive Oil, *page 161*
Roasted Peaches with Cinnamon Basil Sour Cream, *page 170*

Spinach and Eggs

Warm Spinach Salad with Basil and Pine Nuts, *page 148*

Blossom Frittata, *page 149*, with Sautéed Cherry Tomatoes with Marjoram,
    page 164

Fresh Mint Ice Cream, *page 167*

One-Bowl Dinner

Red Quinoa Salad with Upland Cress, Arugula, Avocado, and Plums, *page 144*

Chickpeas with Tomatoes, Feta, and Herbs, *page 150*

Charentais Melon in Coconut Milk, *page 166*

Lamb Chops with Friends

Summer Special Salad, *page 146*

Lamb Chops with Cilantro-Mint Yogurt Dressing, *page 152*

Braised Romano Beans with Tomato and Preserved Lemon, *page 159*

Roasted Potatoes and Fennel with Niçoise Olives, *page 164*

Strawberries and Tarragon Cream, *page 172*

Brunch with Herbs

Mixed Garden Lettuces with Lemon-Oregano Vinaigrette, *page 141*

Fines Herbes Omelet, *page 151*

Squash Blossoms with Ricotta, Mint, and Pepitas, *page 165*

Plum Basil Galette, *page 168*

• RESOURCES •

Internet Sources for Seeds and Plants

Abundant Life Seeds
abundantlifeseeds.com
Everything for yard and garden

Baker Creek Heirloom Seeds
rareseeds.com
*Open-pollinated, pure, natural, non-GMO
    seeds*

Franchi Seeds
growitalian.com
Italian seed company

Graines Baumaux
graines-baumaux.fr
French seed company

Ed Hume Seeds
humeseeds.com
*Especially for the Pacific Northwest,
    specializing in seeds for short seasons
    and cool climates*

Irish Eyes-Garden City Seeds
irisheyesgardenseeds.com
Especially for the High Plains

John Scheepers Kitchen Garden Seeds
kitchengardenseeds.com

Johnny's Selected Seeds
johnnyseeds.com
Especially for the Northeast

Kitazawa Seed Company
kitazawaseed.com
Especially for Asian varieties

Native Seeds
nativeseeds.org
Ancient seeds especially for the Southwest

Richter's Herbs
richters.com
*Herb plants, seeds, books, dried herbs,
    and more*

Ronniger Potato Farm
ronnigers.com
*Certified seed potatoes with varieties
    originating from around the world and
    the United States*

Seeds for the South

seedsforthesouth.com

Vegetable and herb seeds especially for the Southern gardens in Zones 7 to 9

Seeds of Change

seedsofchange.com

Dedicated to preserving biodiversity and promoting sustainable, organic agriculture

Seed Savers Exchange

seedsavers.org

Nonprofit organization of gardeners dedicated to saving and sharing heirloom seeds

Seeds Trust

seedstrust.com

Vegetable, wildflower, native grass, and herb seeds especially for high altitudes

Southern Exposure Seed Exchange

southernexposure.com

Heirloom and other open-pollinated (non-hybrid) seeds especially for the South

Territorial Seed Company

territorialseed.com

Especially for the Pacific Northwest

Thomas Jefferson Center for Historic Plants

monticello.org

Underwood Gardens

underwoodgardens.com

Heirloom vegetable seeds

Internet Sources for Equipment and Supplies

The Farmstead

gardenraisedbeds.com

Gardener's Supply Company

gardeners.com

Peaceful Valley Farm and Garden

groworganic.com

Planet Natural

planetnatural.com

Internet Sources for Cooperative Extension Offices and Farmers' Markets

To find your local Cooperative Extension office:

csrees.usda.gov/Extension/

To find local farmers' markets:

localharvest.org

· RECOMMENDED READING ·

Bartholemew, Mel. *Square Foot Gardening*. Emmaus, PA: Rodale Inc., 2005.

Bradley, Fern Marshall. *Rodale's Vegetable Garden Problem Solver*. Emmaus, PA: Rodale Inc., 2007.

Bradley, Fern Marshall, Barbara W. Ellis, and Ellen Phillips. *Rodale's Ultimate Encyclopedia of Organic Gardening*. Emmaus, PA: Rodale Inc., 2009.

Cunningham, Sally Jean. *Great Garden Companions*. Emmaus, PA: Rodale Inc., 1998.

Coleman, Eliot. *The Four-Season Harvest*. White River Junction, VT: Chelsea Green Publishing Company, 1999.

Creasy, Rosalind. *The Edible Salad Garden*. Boston: Periplus Editions, 1999.

Ellis, Barbara W., and Fern Marshall Bradley. *The Organic Gardener's Handbook of Natural Pest and Disease Control*. Emmaus, PA: Rodale Inc., 2010.

Lanza, Patricia. *Lasagna Gardening*. Emmaus, PA: Rodale Inc., 1998.

Martin, Deborah L., and Grace Gershuny. *The Rodale Book of Composting*. Emmaus, PA: Rodale Inc., 1992.

McGee, Rose Marie Nichols, and Maggie Stuckey. *McGee & Stuckey's Bountiful Container*. New York: Workman, 2002.

Ogden, Shepherd. *Step by Step Organic Vegetable Gardening*. New York: HarperCollins Publishers, 1992.

Olkowski, William, Helga Olkowski, and Sheila Daar. *Common-Sense Pest Control*. Newtown, CT: Taunton Press, 1991.

Page, Karen, and Andrew Dornenburg. *The Flavor Bible*. New York: Little, Brown and Company, 2008.

Proulx, E. Annie. *The Fine Art of Salad Gardening*. Emmaus, PA: Rodale Inc., 1982.

Rice, Graham. *All-in-One Garden*. London: Cassell Illustrated, 2006.

• ACKNOWLEDGMENTS •

I am grateful to the many people who helped make this book possible. Very special thanks to Caroline Greeven, who helped develop the concept; to Karen Bolesta, who patiently guided me every step of the way; to Jeff Spurrier, who turned my ideas into prose; and to everyone at Rodale who made this book clear, accessible, and beautiful!

Heartfelt thanks to RAS for his kindness, love, and support throughout.

• INDEX •

Boldface page references indicate illustrations. <u>Underscored</u> references indicate boxed text.

Access to garden, ease of, 7, 11-12
Appetizers
    Baked Cannellini Beans with
        Tomato, Feta, and Dill Pesto,
        134
    Chilled Cucumber-Avocado Soup
        with Borage Blossoms,
        135
    Grilled Broccoli Rabe, Burrata, and
        Oregano Pizza, 135-36
    Melon and Prosciutto, 137
    Roasted Feta with Honey and
        Thyme, 137
    Roasted Garlic, 138
    Romesco Sauce, 139
    Sweet Corn Soup with Sage Brown
        Butter, 140
Artichokes, 51-53, <u>52</u>
    Braised Baby Artichokes, 156-57
Arugula, 85
    Linguine with Arugula Pecan
        Pesto, 153
    Pole Bean Salad, 142
    Red Quinoa Salad with Upland
        Cress, Arugula, Avocado,
        and Plums, 144
    Shaved Fennel Salad with Arugula,
        Avocado, and Almonds,
        145
    Summer Special Salad, 146
Asparagus, 53-54, **53**, <u>54</u>
    Roasted Asparagus, 163-64

Basil, 94-95
    Eggplant with Herbed Bread
        Crumbs and Pine Nuts, 160
    Melon and Prosciutto, 137
    Plum Basil Galette, 168-69
    Pole Bean Salad, 142
    Roasted Peaches with Cinnamon
        Basil Sour Cream, 170
    Warm Spinach Salad with Basil and
        Pine Nuts, 148
Beans, 55-56, **159**
    Baked Cannellini Beans with
        Tomato, Feta, and Dill Pesto,
        134
    Braised Romano Beans with
        Tomato and Preserved
        Lemon, 159
    Chickpeas with Tomatoes, Feta,
        and Herbs, 150
    Pole Bean Salad, 142
Books, gardening, 177
Borage, 105, **105**
    Chilled Cucumber-Avocado Soup
        with Borage Blossoms, 135
    Summer Special Salad, 146
Broccoli rabe, 58-60, **58**, 128
    Grilled Broccoli Rabe, Burrata, and
        Oregano Pizza, 135-36
Brussels sprouts, 56-58, **56**, **58**, 128
    Braised Brussels Sprouts with
        Bacon, Garlic, and Cider
        Vinegar, 157

Cabbage, 60-62, <u>61</u>, **146**
    Spicy Slaw, 145-46
Calendula, 105-6, **106**
    Basmati Rice with Spices,
        Pistachios, and Calendula,
        156
Carrots, 128
Chard, 62-63
    Braised Rainbow Chard on Toast,
        158-59
Chervil, 95, **95**
    Fines Herbes Omelet, 151
Chicory
    Roasted Chicken Salad with Celery,
        Herbs, and Croutons, 154
    Warm Chicory Salad with Bacon,
        Pepitas, and Sherry Wine
        Vinaigrette, 147
Chives, 96, **122**
    Chilled Cucumber-Avocado Soup
        with Borage Blossoms,
        135
    Fines Herbes Omelet, 151
    Fingerling Potatoes with Chive Oil,
        161
    Little Gem Salad with Sorrel
        Dressing, 141
Cilantro, 96-97, <u>96</u>, **150**
    Chickpeas with Tomatoes, Feta,
        and Herbs, 150
    Grilled Flank Steak with
        Chimichurri, 151-52

Cilantro (contd.)
    Lamb Chops with Cilantro-Mint
        Yogurt Dressing, 152-53
    Spicy Slaw, 145-46
Clovers, **130**, 131
Companion planting method, 2,
    36-38, **37**, **38**, 121-22
Compost/composting
    defining, 26
    green/brown materials and, 29
    heat and, 30
    historical perspective of, 27
    materials to avoid, 30
    methods, 28-33, 29
    moisture and, 30
    raised beds and, 26-28
    smell and, 30
    soil and, 21, 26-27
    space for, 12
    stages of, **31**
    using, 33
Container gardens
    advantages of, 9, **9**
    intensive planting and, 14
    plan, **48**
    soil for, 25-26
    space for, 18
    types of containers for, 18-20, **19**
    watering, 111
Cool-weather plantings, 128-29
Coriander, 96
    Basmati Rice with Spices,
        Pistachios, and Calendula,
        156
    Grilled Flank Steak with
        Chimichurri, 151-52
    Watermelon with Feta, Cracked
        Coriander, and Fennel Seeds,
        148
Corn
    Pole Bean Salad, 142
    Sweet Corn Soup with Sage Brown
        Butter, 140
Cover crops, 130-31, **130**
Crop rotation, 123-24
Cucumbers, 63-65, **63**, 64
    Chilled Cucumber-Avocado Soup
        with Borage Blossoms,
        135
    Summer Special Salad, 146

Dandelion, 85, **85**
Desserts
    Blackberry and Lemon Sorbet, 166
    Charentais Melon in Coconut Milk,
        166
    Fresh Mint Ice Cream, 167

Lavender and Honey Ice Cream,
    167-68
Plum Basil Galette, 168-69
Roasted Peaches with Cinnamon
    Basil Sour Cream, 170
Rosemary Brown Sugar Butter
    Cookies, 170-71
Sage Corn Bread Pudding, 171-72
Strawberries and Tarragon Cream,
    172
Dill, 97
    Baked Cannellini Beans with
        Tomato, Feta, and Dill Pesto,
        134
    Little Gem Salad with Sorrel
        Dressing, 141
    Peas with Bacon, Shallots, Butter,
        and Dill, 163
    Roasted Chicken Salad with Celery,
        Herbs, and Croutons, 154
Direct-to-garden composting method,
    31-32
Diseases. See Pests/diseases
Diversity in garden, 34-35
Drainage, 11
Dressings. See Salads/dressings

Eggplant, 65-67, 66, 115
    Eggplant with Herbed Bread
        Crumbs and Pine Nuts, 160
Endive, 85, **85**
Evaluating garden after one season,
    128

Fall/winter garden plan, **47**
Fennel, 67-68, **67**, 68
    Roasted Potatoes and Fennel with
        Niçoise Olives, 164
    Shaved Fennel Salad with Arugula,
        Avocado, and Almonds, 145
    Watermelon with Feta, Cracked
        Coriander, and Fennel Seeds,
        148
Fertilizing, 112
Flowers, edible, 105. See also specific
    type
Fruits. See specific type

Garlic, 68-71, 70, 129, **138**
    Baked Cannellini Beans with
        Tomato, Feta, and Dill Pesto,
        134
    Braised Baby Artichokes, 156-57
    Braised Brussels Sprouts with
        Bacon, Garlic, and Cider
        Vinegar, 157

Braised Rainbow Chard on Toast,
    158-59
Braised Romano Beans with
    Tomato and Preserved
    Lemon, 159
Chickpeas with Tomatoes, Feta,
    and Herbs, 150
Eggplant with Herbed Bread
    Crumbs and Pine Nuts, 160
Grilled Broccoli Rabe, Burrata, and
    Oregano Pizza, 135-36
Grilled Flank Steak with
    Chimichurri, 151-52
Lamb Chops with Cilantro-Mint
    Yogurt Dressing, 152-53
Lemon-Oregano Vinaigrette,
    141
Linguine with Arugula Pecan
    Pesto, 153
Little Gem Salad with Sorrel
    Dressing, 141
Mustard Greens with Cumin Seeds,
    162
Roast Chicken with Savory, 155
Roasted Garlic, 138
Romesco Sauce, 139
Sautéed Tomatoes with Marjoram,
    164-65
Warm Spinach Salad with Basil and
    Pine Nuts, 148
Germination, poor, 44
Growing seasons, 42
Guiding principles of garden, 2-6

Harvesting, 114-15, 115
Herbs, 94, 94. See also specific type

Insects, 118-20, **119**, 122-23
Intensive planting method, 2, 3-4, **3**,
    14, 35-38
Interplanting method, 2, 35

Kale, 71-72, 72, 128
    Raw Kale Salad with Hazelnuts,
        Blue Cheese, and Black
        Mission Figs, 143-44

    gardening method, 24, **25**
Lavender, 97-98, **168**
    Lavender and Honey Ice Cream,
        167-68
Leeks, 72-74
    Braised Leeks, 158
Lettuce, 85, 128
    Little Gem Salad with Sorrel
        Dressing, 141

Location of garden
  access and, ease of, 7, 11-12
  considerations in, various, 7-8,
    12-13
  space and, 8-10, **8**, **9**
  sunlight and, 7, 10-11
  water and, 7, 11

Main courses
  Blossom Frittata, 149
  Chickpeas with Tomatoes, Feta,
    and Herbs, 150
  Fines Herbes Omelet, 151
  Grilled Flank Steak with
    Chimichurri, 151-52
  Lamb Chops with Cilantro-Mint
    Yogurt Dressing, 152-53
  Linguine with Arugula Pecan
    Pesto, 153
  Roast Chicken with Savory, 155
  Roasted Chicken Salad with Celery,
    Herbs, and Croutons, 154
Maintaining garden
  daily visits to, 6, 108-9
  fertilizing, 112
  fungal disease prevention and, 120
  harvesting, 114-15, <u>115</u>
  off-season, 127-32
  pruning, 112-14
  staking, 112-14, **114**
  time involved in, 108-9
  watering, 7, 11, 109-12, **110**, <u>111</u>
Manure, 22-23, <u>23</u>
Marjoram, 98, **98**
  Sautéed Tomatoes with Marjoram,
    164-65
Materials for garden, 3-4
Melons, 74-76, <u>74</u>
  Charentais Melon in Coconut Milk,
    166
  Melon and Prosciutto, 137
  Summer Special Salad, 146
  Watermelon with Feta, Cracked
    Coriander, and Fennel Seeds,
    148
Mint, 98-99
  Braised Baby Artichokes, 156-57
  Chickpeas with Tomatoes, Feta,
    and Herbs, 150
  Fresh Mint Ice Cream, 167
  Lamb Chops with Cilantro-Mint
    Yogurt Dressing, 152-53
  Spicy Slaw, 145-46
  Squash Blossoms with Ricotta,
    Mint, and Pepitas, 165
  Summer Special Salad, 146

Mizuna, 85, **85**
Mustard greens, 76-78, **77**
  Mustard Greens with Cumin Seeds,
    162

Nasturtiums, 106, <u>106</u>
  Blossom Frittata, 149
Nutrients and nutrient deficiencies,
  112, 117-18

Off-season maintenance, 127-32
Oregano, 99
  Grilled Broccoli Rabe, Burrata, and
    Oregano Pizza, 135-36
  Lemon-Oregano Vinaigrette, 141

Parsley, 100, <u>100</u>
  Braised Baby Artichokes, 156-57
  Braised Romano Beans with
    Tomato and Preserved
    Lemon, 159
  Chickpeas with Tomatoes, Feta,
    and Herbs, 150
  Eggplant with Herbed Bread
    Crumbs and Pine Nuts, 160
  Fines Herbes Omelet, 151
  Grilled Flank Steak with
    Chimichurri, 151-52
  Raw Kale Salad with Hazelnuts,
    Blue Cheese, and Black
    Mission Figs, 143-44
  Roasted Chicken Salad with Celery,
    Herbs, and Croutons, 154
Parsnips, 128
Patterns, planting, **57**, **59**
Peaches, 78-79
  Roasted Peaches with Cinnamon
    Basil Sour Cream, 170
Peas
  Peas with Bacon, Shallots, Butter,
    and Dill, 163
Peppers, 80-81
  Romesco Sauce, 139
Pests/diseases
  animal, 12, 125-26
  balance and, 116-17
  club root, 120
  common, 118-20, **119**
  companion planting method and,
    121-22
  crop rotation and, 123-24
  fungi, 120
  insects, 118-20, **119**, 122-23
  mildew, downy, 120
  noticing, 117
  nutrient deficiencies and, 117-18

  organic controls for, 124-25
  rodents, 12, 125
  sanitation and, 120-21
  water stress and, 117
Plans, garden, 45, **46-49**
Planting goals, 2-3
Planting times, 42
Potatoes, 81-83, **81**, 128
  Fingerling Potatoes with Chive Oil,
    161
  Roasted Potatoes and Fennel with
    Niçoise Olives, 164
  Sweet Corn Soup with Sage Brown
    Butter, 140
Produce, 1-2, 6. *See also specific type*
Pruning, **63**, **91**, 112-14, 132

Radicchio, 85
  Radicchio and Violet Salad, 143
Rainwater, collecting, <u>110</u>
Raised beds
  advantages of, 15
  building, 15-18, **17**, <u>18</u>
  compost/composting and, 26-28
  intensive planting and, 14
  soil for, 21-25
Recipes. *See specific ingredient*
Resources, gardening, 175-77
Rock powders, <u>24</u>
Rosemary, 100-101
  Rosemary Brown Sugar Butter
    Cookies, 170-71

Sage, 101
  Sage Corn Bread Pudding, 171-72
  Sweet Corn Soup with Sage Brown
    Butter, 140
Salad greens, 83-86, **85**
Salads/dressings
  harvesting leafy greens for, <u>115</u>
  Lemon-Oregano Vinaigrette, 141
  Little Gem Salad with Sorrel
    Dressing, 141
  Pole Bean Salad, 142
Salads/dressings
  Racicchio and Violet Salad, 143
  Raw Kale Salad with Hazelnuts,
    Blue Cheese, and Black
    Mission Figs, 143-44
  Red Quinoa Salad with Upland
    Cress, Arugula, Avocado,
    and Plums, 144
  Shaved Fennel Salad with Arugula,
    Avocado, and Almonds, 145
  Spicy Slaw, 145-46
  Summer Special Salad, 146

Salads/dressings (contd.)
  Warm Chicory Salad with Bacon,
    Pepitas, and Sherry Wine
    Vinaigrette, 147
  Warm Spinach Salad with Basil and
    Pine Nuts, 148
  Watermelon with Feta, Cracked
    Coriander, and Fennel Seeds,
    148
Sanitation, good, 120-21
Savory, 102, **102**
  Pole Bean Salad, 142
  Roast Chicken with Savory, 155
Seasonal menus, 173-74. See also
    specific course
Seeds/seedlings
  collecting, 34
  disease-resistant, 41
  germination, poor, 44
  hybrid, 41
  packet labels, reading, 41-42
  regional planting times and, 42
  saving, 129
  soil for, 42
  sowing, 43-45, **44**
  space for, 12-13
  transplants versus, 38-39
  variety selections, 39-41
Shady border garden plan, **49**
Shallots, 86-87, **86**
  Peas with Bacon, Shallots, Butter,
    and Dill, 163
  Raw Kale Salad with Hazelnuts,
    Blue Cheese, and Black
    Mission Figs, 143-44
  Roasted Chicken Salad with Celery,
    Herbs, and Croutons, 154
  Warm Chicory Salad with Bacon,
    Pepitas, and Sherry Wine
    Vinaigrette, 147
Side dishes
  Basmati Rice with Spices,
    Pistachios, and Calendula, 156
  Braised Baby Artichokes, 156-57
  Braised Brussels Sprouts with
    Bacon, Garlic, and Cider
    Vinegar, 157
  Braised Leeks, 158
  Braised Rainbow Chard on Toast,
    158-59
  Braised Romano Beans with
    Tomato and Preserved
    Lemon, 159
  Eggplant with Herbed Bread
    Crumbs and Pine Nuts, 160

Fingerling Potatoes with Chive Oil,
    161
  Heirloom Tomatoes with Warm
    Butter and Thyme, 162
  Mustard Greens with Cumin Seeds,
    162
  Peas with Bacon, Shallots, Butter,
    and Dill, 163
  Roasted Asparagus, 163-64
  Roasted Potatoes and Fennel with
    Niçoise Olives, 164
  Sautéed Cherry Tomatoes with
    Marjoram, 164-65
  Squash Blossoms with Ricotta,
    Mint, and Pepitas, 165
Soil
  compost/composting and, 21,
    26-27
  for container gardens, 25-26
  importance of, 21
  lasagna gardening method and,
    24, **25**
  manure and, 22-23, 23
  for raised beds, 21-25
  replenishing, 131-32
  rock powders and, 24
  for seeds/seedlings, 42
  testing, 26
Sorrel, 102-3, **102**
  Little Gem Salad with Sorrel
    Dressing, 141
Sowing seeds/seedlings, 43-45, **44**
Space, creative use of, 8-10, **8**, **9**
Spinach, 87-88, 128
  Warm Spinach Salad with Basil and
    Pine Nuts, 148
Squash, 88-90, 89
  Squash Blossoms with Ricotta,
    Mint, and Pepitas, 165
Stable bedding, 23-24
Staking, 112-14, **114**
Summer garden plan, 45, **46**
Sunlight, 7, 10-11

Tarragon, 103
  Fines Herbes Omelet, 151
  Roasted Chicken Salad with Celery,
    Herbs, and Croutons, 154
  Strawberries and Tarragon Cream,
    172
Three Sisters planting method, 37
Thyme, 103-4, 103
  Blackberry and Lemon Thyme
    Sorbet, 166
  Braised Leeks, 158

Heirloom Tomatoes with Warm
    Butter and Thyme, 162
  Roasted Feta with Honey and
    Thyme, 137
  Roasted Garlic, 138
Tomatoes, 45, 90-93, **91**, **92**
  Baked Cannellini Beans with
    Tomato, Feta, and Dill Pesto,
    134
  Braised Rainbow Chard on Toast,
    158-59
  Braised Romano Beans with
    Tomato and Preserved
    Lemon, 159
  Chickpeas with Tomatoes, Feta,
    and Herbs, 150
  Heirloom Tomatoes with Warm
    Butter and Thyme, 162
  Pole Bean Salad, 142
  Romesco Sauce, 139
  Sautéed Tomatoes with Marjoram,
    164-65
Tools, gardening, 13
Transition of garden from summer to
    winter, 127-28
Transplants, 38-39, 43-45
Trap crops, 121-22, 121, **122**
Trellising, 113-14, **114**
Turnips, 128
Two-bin composting method, 28-31,
    29

Upland cress, 85, **85**
  Red Quinoa Salad with Upland
    Cress, Arugula, Avocado,
    and Plums, 144
  Roasted Chicken Salad with Celery,
    Herbs, and Croutons, 154

Vegetables, 50-51, 129. See also
    specific type
Vertical growth of plants, **8**
Violets, 107
  Radicchio and Violet Salad, 143

Water stress, 111, 117
Water/watering, 7, 11, 109-12, **110**, 111,
    132
Wind, 12
Worm bins, 32-33

Zucchini, 115